ASTROLOGY FOR BEGINNERS

The Survival Guide to Discover Yourself Using Horoscope and Zodiac Signs. How to Manage Your Destiny, Master Your Life and Spiritual Growth through Astrology, Tarot, Numerology, and Enneagram

By Lisa Woods

Contents

Introduction 4
Chapter 1. Astrology Throughout the Ages (History) 8
Chapter 2. Astrology and the Planet 11
Chapter 3. Horoscopes 15
Chapter 4. The 12 Zodiac Signs and their Meanings 19
Chapter 5. The Birth Chart 23
Chapter 6. The Ascendant 27
Chapter 7. Tarot the History 32
Chapter 8. Tarot Cards and their Meanings 37
Chapter 9. Numerology, what is it? 42
Chapter 10. How to Calculate your Numerology and What it Means? 46
Chapter 11. The Significance of Names 49
Chapter 12. Fibonacci Numbers 52
Chapter 13. What is Enneagram– Harmony Triads and Nine Types 56
Chapter 14. How to Master the Spiritual Growth 61
Chapter 15. Aquarius, Pisces, Aries and Taurus 64
Chapter 16. Gemini, Cancer, Leo, Virgo, Libra, Scorpio, Sagittarius and Capricorn 68
Chapter 17. Celestial Sphere 76
Chapter 18. How each Planet's Astrology Directly Affects every Zodiac Sign 79
Chapter 19. Oracle Cards and Psycards 84
Chapter 20. Performing Tarot Readings 87
Chapter 21. Note for Readings for Others 90
Chapter 22. Tarot 101- Getting Started 93
Chapter 23. Decks for Experienced Readers, Collectors, and Tarot Lovers 97
Chapter 24. The Effect of Numerology on Your Life 102
Chapter 25. How to Read Astrological Chart 105

Chapter 26.	True Purpose of the Zodiac Sign in Life	109
Chapter 27.	Expression Number	114
Chapter 28.	Life Paths	118
Chapter 29.	Kundalini	123
Chapter 30.	Kundalini Yoga Poses	128
Chapter 31.	The Language of Energy	131
Chapter 32.	The Test Enneagram Instructions	133
Chapter 33.	Decoding the Nine-Value Code	138
Conclusion		142

Text Copyright © Lisa Woods

All rights reserved. No part of this guide may be reproduced in any form without permission in writing from the publisher except in the case of brief quotations embodied in critical articles or reviews.

Legal & Disclaimer

The information contained in this book and its contents is not designed to replace or take the place of any form of medical or professional advice; and is not meant to replace the need for independent medical, financial, legal or other professional advice or services, as may be required. The content and information in this book have been provided for educational and entertainment purposes only.

The content and information contained in this book have been compiled from sources deemed reliable, and it is accurate to the best of the Author's knowledge, information and belief. However, the Author cannot guarantee its accuracy and validity and cannot be held liable for any errors and/or omissions. Further, changes are periodically made to this book as and when needed. Where appropriate and/or necessary, you must consult a professional (including but not limited to your doctor, attorney, financial advisor or such other professional advisor) before using any of the suggested remedies, techniques, or information in this book.

Upon using the contents and information contained in this book, you agree to hold harmless the Author from and against any damages, costs, and expenses, including any legal fees potentially resulting from the application of any of the information provided by this book. This disclaimer applies to any loss, damages or injury caused by the use and application, whether directly or indirectly, of any advice or information presented, whether for breach of contract, tort, negligence, personal injury, criminal intent, or under any other cause of action.

You agree to accept all risks of using the information presented inside this book.

You agree that by continuing to read this book, where appropriate and/or necessary, you shall consult a professional (including but not limited to your doctor, attorney, or financial advisor or such other advisor as needed) before using any of the suggested remedies, techniques, or information in this book.

Introduction

Our Universe came into existence with the help of Sun, Moon, Stars and other Celestial bodies. Astrology is a science that studies about the association between the positions of the sun, moon, stars and other celestial bodies and human beings. Astrology, in its broadest sense, is the search for human meaning in the sky. Human beings living on planet Earth looked upwards at the sky to know directions and answers for their life occurrences. Over 25,000 years ago people realized that the moon influenced the tides, oceans and seas. As time passed people realized that the change in night sky did have an influence over humans and they started to look at celestial bodies to seek answers. The cosmic dance that is happening always in the sky is looked upon to get answers for our lives on earth and that study of metaphysics is known as astrology. It is a study that is beyond physical that involves intuition and psychic powers. Astrology is also known as the 'mother of all sciences'.

Before the advent of electricity, people used sunrise and moonlight to calculate days and time. The impact of stars, planets and the moon on plant and animal behavior on earth has been well documented. The indents appearing on animals were taken as symbols and messages from God. The Gods also presented themselves in images and stars with whom they were associated. Even evil stars were associated with a particular planet indicating dissatisfaction or disturbance or adverse events. Such indications were dealt with by appeasing the Gods and found ways to please the Gods so that nothing negative begot the king or ruler. Omens and magic were believed by the rulers of that era.

Ancient temples and architecture were built with sophisticated awareness of celestial cycles. Astrological predictions have been accepted as a science and increasingly further studies and research is being conducted to distil and fine tune the methods and processes. Critics are of the opinion that how can you categorize the entire world population into 12 signs? Well, broadly it is done and that is how astrology can help to determine a person's nature and foretell his future. We all believe that there are energies present within us as well as in the universe. If both are in tune with each other that is when the universe showers us with abundance. This is the fundamental secret of the 'Law of Attraction'. Using this base the time when a person is born is recorded on the celestial clock along with the position of the stars and planets at that point of time in the vast sky. With the position of the Sun, Moon and other planets at the time of birth an individual's birth chart or horoscope is devised and looked into. A professional astrologer, who has learnt the science along with loads of intuition, combines his powers to predict what sort of a person the individual is and how his life on this planet will be.

Numerology, astrology, and tarot all connect together. Each of these divinity reading styles have their own unique way that they fit together with the other two, yet they all come together to develop a persuasive reading format for all. If you have ever been drawn to astrology or tarot, chances are you will be surprised to learn that numerology is not too different from these two reading styles. Read on to learn more about how they all connect together.

Astrology Throughout the Ages

Ancient Astrology

Many great men like Copernicus Galileo, Ptolemy, and Aristotle were some of the early astrologers who stirred in the minds of many other thinkers what the stars and planets may hold and what they tell us. These celestial shifts and movements fascinated others after them to ask more questions about what is beyond our planet so much so that astronomy was once a subject of science. The many suppositions of these great thinkers would eventually pave the way for people to use their imaginings in a way that would allow us to contradict, answer, give solutions and reveal information.

They were not the only ones who had great ideas about the universe and the planets and stars it holds but It was them and others like them who stirred the minds of many other intellectuals throughout time, time and again, to challenge or solidify their initial ideas. Astrology, in a grand gesture of providing knowledge of what is seen in the heavens, allowed the expansion of the study of the universe, man, and his being, as well as other disciplines of science that give us the luxuries and technologies we enjoy today. Many of what were once imagined and fathomed only in the recesses of the mind of man, are now realities in our lives. What once was thought to be only possible in fantasy has become a reality because of the initial work and documentation of sky observers of the past.

But it was also because of those advancements that gave way to more critical questions about the reality and accuracy of what astrology claims to bring to the table. And because it has been so widely misunderstood for what it stands and what it imparts, it had lost its luster and dulled the interests of many when claims relating to and about astrology were made. However, there was always a small minority of individuals who continued to study astrology and adjusted their perceptions to open up a broader more expansive knowledge of it.

The mathematical aspect of this science was dug into more profound and secretly studied by many when others were persecuted, imprisoned and others even put to death because of the information they shared - sometimes a complete false, other times accurate, while there are theories earlier refuted but later (much later) was proven to be true.

Astrology is a set of principles that if followed, practiced, conveyed and understood correctly, tells us of our place under the sun and essentially helps us explain situations and events in our lives. It does not take away free will from us nor does invoke to have an individual believe that they have no choice and "it is written in the stars". Astrology aims to further the knowledge of oneself with one's own using the knowledge man has gained according to the planets and stars pull on our inner being. It aims to shed light on you, as an individual A guide, if you may, to assist you at any given time of your life.

Modern Astrology

The fast movement of scientific knowledge recently has seen significant advancement in terms of machinery and tools that allows us the modern conveniences we have that many of us take for granted. Many of these inventions and tools of the many branches of the sciences are much owed to many individuals of long bygone history whose imaginings went far beyond their space and realm of time. Because of all these we are now able to enjoy many perks and advantages not available to those who came before us.

Astrology may have waned in the interest and curiosity of people by the 17th century but had picked up interest anew when the 1970's rolled around. There are presently a few schools around the world that teach Astrology to students curious about the craft and discipline of the study. To further the institution of astrology, schools have not only streamlined the practice, but have also gone so far as to certify individuals who have passed the standards founded on the study. The advent of these formal schools and eventual certification gives credence to the fact that astrology is and will be a system of looking at their circumstances, events and situations from a higher perspective, if you must.

Today's technology has contributed to the clarity of what astronomy is and has given astrologers a better perception of the relation of planets and stars to the daily events and circumstances of individuals. Because of the significant advancement of our knowledge about the universe, the discovery of "new" planets has allowed astrology to compartmentalize and able to generalize readings, i.e. when is the best date and times to officially open that coffee and pastry shop you've always wanted.

Back then an astrologer's job was a tedious one of creating a chart - and you shall have a good idea of the time spent on this as we shall go over making one later. A chart takes precision and mathematical calculations in order to get all the quantifiers in alignment. It took a lot of sheets of paper, elbow grease, and careful thought to measurements to come up with an accurate chart. Nowadays, technological modernity has allowed

Computers, and computer software has allowed astrologers the convenience of having a software create a chart based on information given by an individual, but it would still take a practicing or seasoned astrologer to read those charts and interpret them using the methods and applying the principles of the discipline they have learnt. This is where the human touch remains. Here is when the astrologer is present for any questions an individual may have. Here is where the astrologer can tell you what you can't decipher for yourself.

Astrology and the Planet

The astrology is focused on stars, signs, aspects, and buildings. For the purpose of predicting or concentrating on a specific branch of astrology, many more rates and interpretation resources can be added. The set stars and constellations form an ancient branch of astrology and come back promptly now. Many stars and constellations appear behind the planets on the map, and can also be interpreted as a rich context that helps to identify specific life problems more accurately.

Karmic and mystical astrology focuses on the person's soul and his rebirth in this particular life and looks at the past karmas and lessons to be learned.

Astrology is prevalent for relationships, and this approach is called synastry. The diagrams and interactions of two or more individuals are collected, providing a rich insight into the way they communicate, whether they be friends, partners, family members, or colleagues. It can be helpful in identifying potential barriers and communication problems and supporting each other. It can demonstrate how far a relationship is going to go and if there is more to it than sex.

The forecasting is a tool that can be used with high precision in astrology because we know potential celestial motions. This can show us today's and future forces in our lives and help us with things such as: Is this a good time for me to find a new job? Should I sustain my relationship, or is it time to pursue my own path? Why is life currently so complicated, throwing obstacles after obstacles? Would my health improve or deteriorate, and what remedies are possible? Will I travel around the world or stay at home? It is important to remember that a reading of astrology will never govern. Your own choice is what you do. It also does not predict things such as death, since the astrologer is ethical and cannot be explicitly defined. What it can do is give you good times to pursue new ideas or relax and find inspiration. It can show you possibilities-it is up to you how you want to use them. This can illustrate to you why and what the object of the complexity is to be measured and how it can best be transformed.

Once a good astrologer first reads his diagram, he is usually surprised and intrigued by how detailed it is. It's not necessary to understand why it works, although fascinating, because it seems to help people anyway. Astrology is an extremely useful method for guidance and transformation, the course of the soul, and the fundamental questions as to why we are here for all aspects of life and personality.

Uranus is a kind of Saturn's nemesis. The structure breaks down often abruptly or unconventionally. At this point, such variables never need again to be studied, but Uranus is once again opposed (creating conflict and breakdown) to Saturn's systems. A bit of an explosive impact will occur-literally or figuratively. An excellent example is a disaster in the Gulf of Mexico. Fossil fuel dependency is part of an old system that absolutely MUST die. Uranus came in explosively to show this fact to anyone who just didn't. Relationships also experience massive change during the transits of Uranus. The laws (which come from the power of Saturn) shift-often because of sudden death (literally or metaphorically), accident, or because someone broke it without warning! Uranus last opposed Saturn before 2008 in 1965-66-the early years of the Civil Rights movement! Think of social change, social change, and personal systems... Although some of the changes may take us away from the guard, the destruction Uranus still liberates us!

Jupiter expresses our ideals, values, self-worth perception, and capacity to expand on the basis of what we believe is our Supreme truth (physical, financial, spiritual, creative, professional...). Many astrologers name Jupiter, because of its vast existence, the planet of good fortune. Spiritual teachers, teachers, and gurus of healing are an excellent example of Jupiter's higher vibration. Nevertheless, when running in a lower capacity, Jupiter can be just. Religious fanatics are manifestations of Jupiter's lower vibration. In line with Jupiter, Uranus is currently cultivating a new foundation of values and ideals, a lot of religious fanatism, a conflict in the Middle East, a greater interest in new forms of non-denominational spirituality and unorthodox business practices, both of which are evolving and carrying a different level. Consider expanding unorthodox ideologies. This strength is somewhat inappropriate because the two planets are in Aries ' feisty position!

Pluto... I love to talk about Pluto because I feel it's more fascinating than any other planet. Most astrologers do not comprehend Pluto, but it's interesting, I believe! While Pluto ' downgraded' several years ago to asteroid status, its energy remains one of the most concentrated as it retains its potential for death, rebirth, and full transformation. Simple: like a tidal wave, Pluto experiences disasters, and the consequences are dramatic. The psychological action of the surfaces as we navigate the Pluto process gives us our weakest attributes because we can fall into fear and survival... Obsessively, we can go on to exploit, control, or distort our world (including others), trying to cover the hidden truths below the tapestry. The energy can be cumbersome, dark, possessive, sexual, and dependent. What was ground and our true intentions have already hit latent (collectively or individually) are visible the explanation for this? Deep beneath the surface of the psyche are obsessive secrets and attributes which have to be purged and transformed for real evolution. Anything but shallow! Anything less!

Examples of the Plutonian role in our Grand Cross include government and corporate corruption, the mortgage crisis, our addiction to oil and materialism, the abuse of money, natural disasters and the surface disrepute, efforts to manipulate, harass and dominate other people, while lying about real reasons for doing this, many of the tough things that happen in our lives have become difficult to do. Phew! Phew! The Moon is our ego. It includes emotions, self-identity, mechanisms for defense, intuition, projection, physical and psychological sense, as well as our homes, personal relationships, and comfort.

I will only talk briefly to Venus and Mars as they will be part of our Grand Cross for a short time, but their role must be taken into account.

Venus: material ideals, representations of the public, connections with commodities, and how we describe ourselves in our material world.

Mars: rage, expression of oneself, imagination, fighter, male power, ability to act.

Saturn, Uranus, and Pluto will continue to conflict cycling through 2012. Jupiter is going to cycle in and out by March 2011. The Grand Cross would be triggered at a number of times when Moon (or other planets) transits Cancer's sign: 10-11 July 2010 7 August 2010, 3 September 2010 1 October 2010 (slightly less intensive) 30 June-11 July 2011 7-15 July 2011 (with Venus in a Mix and not Earth) 17-18 July 2012 (with Mars in a Mix instead of the Saturn) Remove many planets to the mix and add friction and difficulty. We have to incorporate the following features into this particular series of planetary transits: to yield to the fact that an old paradigm simply does not work and allows us to move with waves of change, rather than to fight against them or try to preserve what does not work, modesty, thinking outside the box. All this refers to the ways in which we perform our relationships, expenses, and medical treatment (I think it right now is useful to explore alternative therapies and incorporate them into West medicine), living arrangements, preferences, assumptions about beliefs, jobs, and everyday decisions. It is equally essential that the nuances of the plot are not lost. Take notice, then, of what is awry and take action. Repeating the misery tale does nothing to change it. Taking action as described above and connecting with your inner guidance helps to change the ball!

You can't move in, out, left, or right without bumping your head against the wall with situations or logistics, but IMAGINE yourself fills your heart with passion, light, and transcending-free from a commitment to specific results-knowing that it's better to stay up and out! Right now, your job is not to confine yourself to practical risks. Instead, it is your time to heal yourself, transform your own energy (experience), and believe in endless expansion opportunities. The duty of Spirit is to look after the data.

Horoscopes

Horoscope is a guide of zodiacal hover with Earth at the middle. The highest point of the circle speaks to the Sun at its most elevated point during the day and left and right of that are the eastern and western skylines.

Your horoscope outlines the overall places of the Sun, moon, planets, and stars at a particular time and spot based on your personal preferences. Celestial prophets don't utilize 'clock time'. Instead, they measure it as "sidereal" time, as estimated from the sun's situation at the spring equinox.

When the date and time are chosen and determined ass sidereal time and the area known and plotted, the soothsayer counsels a galactic ephemeris (a table posting the areas of the Sun, Moon, planets, and groups of the stars at some random time) to develop the graph.

While this used to be repetitive and demanding, P.C. programming have made it very simple. The study of building a graph is just the initial step. Legitimate understanding of the diagram is both a craftsman and a science. Appropriately done, it uncovers characters that have bits of knowledge and current patterns, and should just be endowed to a profoundly prepared and licensed celestial prophet.

Many people may consult astrologers about sorting out a relationship issue, changing jobs or changing careers, opening a new business and becoming self-employed.

People usually make changes to improve their earning potential.

We will look at areas of income that relate to other people's resources — for example, bank loans, business partnerships, inheritance, and gifted money.

We will study the indicators in the natal horoscope. I will be using an example that I have imaginary come up with to illustrate well how Horoscope can change your life even financially. By studying one horoscope, we will clearly see the natal configurations sensitive to career and financial changes.

Let's start with the indicators of financial improvement in the horoscope. We want to see solar arc or transit activity from Jupiter, Uranus or Pluto in 8th harmonic hard aspect -- conjunction, semi square (45 degrees), square, (135 degrees) and opposition - to the ruler of the 2nd house (money) and planets located in the 2nd house. We want to focus as well on the ruler of the 8th house or planets in the 8th house since this area concerns other people's resources.

Jupiter is a beneficial planet. It augments and expands whatever it touches. Uranus represents sudden changes, upsetting the status quo, bringing in new and exciting developments.

And Pluto signifies empowerment and transformation.

We are not interested in transiting Neptune. If for example transiting Neptune is in hard aspect to the planet ruling the 2nd house, it can suggest confusion, doubt, insecurity even deception with finances.

Neptune generally is not going to be a positive influence, as well with Saturn in hard aspect to a planet ruling the 2nd or 8th house. Saturn tends to be controlling and restrictive. So, we want to focus on Jupiter, Uranus and Pluto.

We want to look for solar arcs or transits from Jupiter, Uranus or Pluto in hard aspect to the angles of the horoscope. The Midheaven (MC) reflects a change of status, career developments and recognition. As well, in hard aspect to the planet ruling the 10th house or located in the 10th house. Same for the 11th house as well, since it represents income and recognition from the profession.

Another essential combination in solar arc (SA) or transit activity is Pluto or Uranus to Jupiter, and vice-versa such as Jupiter in hard aspect to Pluto or Uranus, or Pluto in hard aspect to Jupiter, or Uranus in hard aspect to Jupiter.

Jupiter to Uranus or Uranus to Jupiter suggests exciting opportunities, success, becoming independent, and heading to where the grass is greener. It is optimism and intensifies (Uranus) reward (Jupiter). Likewise, Jupiter to Pluto or Pluto to Jupiter symbolizes success, wealth, establishing new perspectives of opportunity, leadership, influence, and resourcefulness.

The reward cycle of transiting Jupiter conjunct the Sun, occurs every twelve years. When you test someone's past through this cycle, you should see a theme reoccurring every twelve years of success or reward.

For example, that I had started a business venture every twelve years.

If transiting Jupiter conjunct the Sun does not manifest as reward, there are usually other mitigating measurements or factors that trump or negate Jupiter. For example, transiting

Pluto to Saturn, or transiting Neptune to the Sun or angle of the horoscope can be challenging.

Usually however, transiting Jupiter conjunct the Sun marks a time of promotion, reward and recognition.

We also want to look for solar arc or transiting Uranus to Saturn. This suggests a wake-up call of ambition. Imagine cheerleaders on the sidelines at a football game, jumping up and down. It's time to get things going, to pick up the pace.

It intensifies ambition, bringing in exciting new developments. It can also suggest making changes that will afford the person more freedom or individuality. Sometimes it can be about freedom in relationships leading to a separation, but at the same time, career developments can coincide. Check your horoscope when solar arc or transiting Uranus was in hard aspect with natal Saturn and see what manifested then.

Perhaps the reason people have a fascination with the skies is because they provide a way to learn about ourselves. There is an ancient saying, "As above – so below." One interpretation of that saying is "Know the universe – know you." It could be said that as human beings are part of nature and inhabitants of the universe, they work by the same laws as the stars. From that perspective, we can learn more about ourselves by studying the larger domain we live in. But still, studying the stars ONLY to get a better grasp about our lives, or ONLY to calculate the best timing for doing one thing or another, misses a higher point. Astrology is far more than that.

In ancient times, the knowledge of the more enormous potential of astrology, beyond just personal decision making, was held by only a few trained individuals. For the people who worked with esoteric astrology, the stars in the sky were not only bright lights or a tool for prediction. For them, astrology was inseparable from their way of life. It was part of their cosmic perception, belief system, and religion.

For example, in ancient Greece (and Rome, which adopted a great deal from Greek culture), stars and gods were one. Therefore, not only did the Greek predict the movement of the planets/gods in the sky, they also tried to influence the planets/gods by building beautiful temples for them, by praying, and by conducting rituals and ceremonies. This might seem to us today as superstitious. But it is based on a profound insight, acknowledging that not only do the planets affect us, but we also can affect the planets and the stars. For the Greeks it was known that a simple prayer or heroic act could make the gods change their decisions and hence change the way a planet will influence one's life. Later on in history we will see practitioners like Culpeper using different herbs to change a particular astrological influence upon a person. But the notion of the reciprocity between the stars and human beings goes much further than that, and touches excellent spiritual truths. There is mutuality between humans and the celestial bodies and the connection does not go one way only.

In many ancient cultures there are references to Astrology – the state of the heavenly bodies. Traveling, or just sitting outside without bright lights, people were exposed to the stars night after night, year after year. They would have watched their journey across the sky. They would have known their names and their orbits.

Native Americans believed that when one of the tribe elders died they turned into a bright star in the sky. They identified some of the stars as essential figures from their past. This demonstrates their belief that humans can develop to be stars, shining forth, and leading the way with their light for others, and also changing the celestial scenery forever.

The 12 Zodiac Signs and their Meanings

Aries

Aries is symbolized by the ram which represents the male fertility as well as courage and aggression. The ram's horn is considered as part of the cornucopia thus it is dubbed as the horn of plenty. People who are born under this sign have the affinity towards abundance.

Sun in Aries people are born as natural athletes. They are active, energetic, straightforward and not complicated. They are people who know what they want and how they can achieve them. On the other hand, the moon can also play a vital role in affecting their behavior. For instance, Moon in Aries people are somewhat impatient thus they live for the moment and hardly has the patience to wait for things to happen. This is the reason why they are proactive in solving their problems because they need to see the results immediately. In general, people who are born under this sign are competitive, quick and direct.

Taurus

Taurus has always been the symbol of strength and power. Taureans are believed to be healthy individuals but although they are dependable because they have the habit of being outright helpful. They are also naturally sensual people in all pleasure areas, and they take delight on just about anything like food, a comfortable blanket and even flowers. Since they revel in things that give them comfort, they also have the tendency to revel in material things. Since they are strong-willed individuals, it is unwise to push people born under this star to do things that they are not committed. However, once they are committed to doing things, they put all their time, energy and effort to doing things. This is the reason why people born under this star are very passionate about love and romance.

Gemini

Gemini are perceived to have dual nature as this sign is symbolized by twins. Gemini love to move around freely and mingle with people to get answers to their questions.

Cancer

Being symbolized by the crab, people who are born under this star always move in indirect manner. They direct their lives towards where they can gain a lot of advantages in their lives. This is the reason why they have strong survival instincts. They are also very protective particularly in sharing their inner selves to many people.

Cancers also have the reputation to be moody. This is evident to those who are born when the Moon is in Cancer. Although withdrawn, people who are born under this zodiac sign are thoughtful by nature. They are also sensitive to love, and they can give a lot of things to their loved ones like security, comfort and care. Overall, Cancers often move about with their business without making a lot of noise. They are gentle people that invest in their inner selves more than anything else.

Leo

The zodiac sign Leo is symbolized by the might lion which represents ruling, courage and sovereignty. In fact, there is an unmistakable regal air to people who are born under this star. They are dignified but they also have the reputation for being conceited.

On the other hand, Leo people also love being the center of attention. Whether they are inside their homes or out with their friends, Leo people want to be always in the spotlight. They also have the incessant need to be in control of things and their all-controlling behavior can be difficult to bear with.

Virgo

Virgo people are, in general, respectable people. The symbol, the virgin, is interpreted as having pure in spirit and also being self-contained. Virgos are reticent especially when they face something new. Virgos find contentment, security and comfort in little things. Having said this, many people under this sign are accused to be underachievers. The satisfaction that they get from simple things prevents them from pursuing great things in life. Although this may be the case, this is the quality of Virgo people that makes them endear.

Libra

The danger for the people with this sign – Financial success is not a priority to Libras, and they will have many ups and downs when it comes to their careers because of this. Libras place more value on peace and justice in their lives.

Scorpio

Scorpios are intense people and they are very determined when it comes to achieving the things that they want to do.

Sagittarius

Sagittarius is people who are outgoing and friendly. The love freedom and they abhor doing routine works. Their love for making friends also puts them at risk because they often have blind faith in people. Their optimism is infectious, but this can also lead them to trouble from time to time. Since Sagittarians are under the fire sign, they also have quick tempers but, fortunately, they quickly forget the source of their anger.

Sagittarians have the need for constant activity and their outgoing personality makes them irresponsible. They quickly forget appointments and they find it challenging to complete tasks that they don't like. Although this may be the case, they can also become good teachers as they are right in storytelling.

Capricorn

People born under this sign are grounded and realistic. Being useful as well as productive is essential for Capricorns because they want to keep their emotions under check.

Aquarius

Aquarius is under the sun sign and people under this zodiac revere the old and traditional ways of doing things. They have strong idealism thus they are likely to have fixed opinions on everything. Unfortunately, this is the reason why most Aquarians are branded as standoffish individuals, but this is just a façade. In reality, they are observant and tolerant in a broad sense. They are also very witty and intellectual people.

Pisces

Pisces contains all experiences of all the zodiac signs. Thus, they have the ability to communicate and identify with people from all backgrounds. They are not only adaptable, but they also have broad minds. Even if they are not sure of their purpose early on, when they find it, they rise to the challenge in a way only a Pisces can.

The Birth Chart

The birth chart or the natal chart is a cosmic blueprint of the soul's incarnation in this lifetime. It shows traits, possibilities, soul lessons, the soul's evolutionary purpose, and more. Contained within that blueprint is you, as reflected in the cosmos. We'll take a look at the individual parts of the chart and what they each mean. If you are familiar with astrology, then it will give you the basics to begin understanding your own chart.

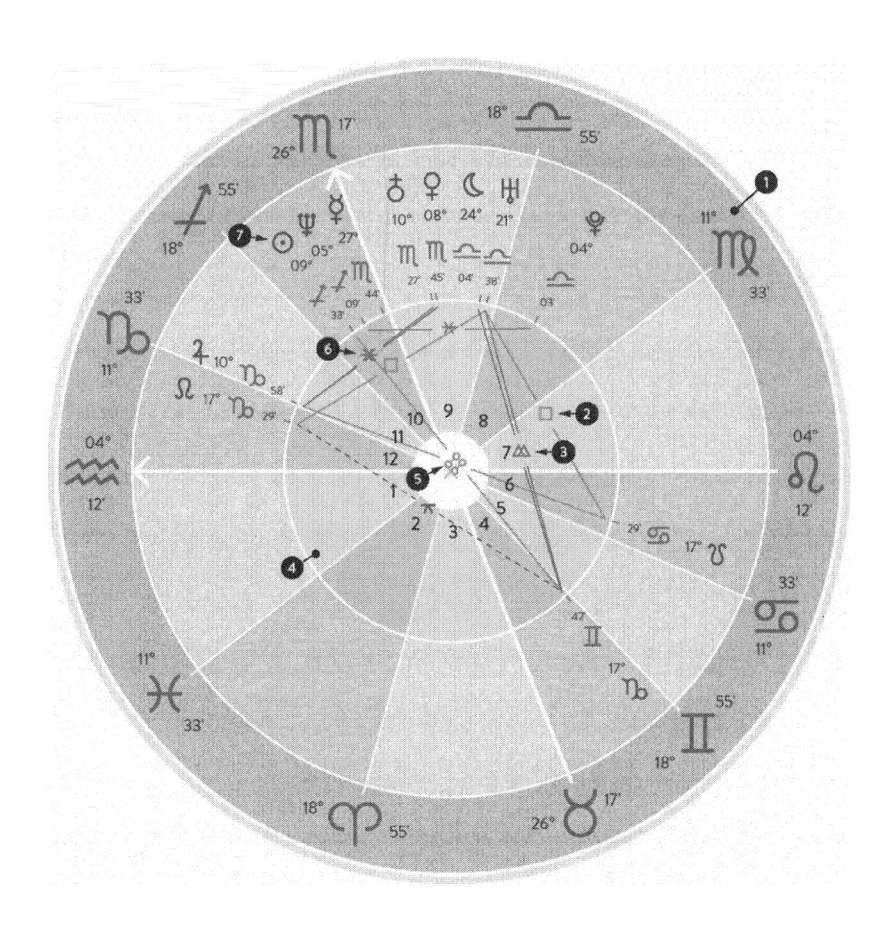

LEGEND: 1. Signs; 2. Square Aspect; 3. Trine Aspect; 4. Houses by number, counterclockwise; 5. Opposition Aspect; 6. Sextile Aspect; 7. Planets

Sample Birth Chart. The chart is a wheel, or mandala, divided into 12 segments, or houses. Each house is ruled by a zodiac sign and represents a specific area of life. The chart shows the placement of planets and other celestial bodies within the zodiac based on the date, time, and location of a person's birth. The connecting lines in the middle are the aspects.

THE SUN

The Sun is our very core or ego; it is both the central organizing principle of the galaxy and our self. Much of our personality is predicated on our Sun sign, which is why the horoscopes you might read online or in periodicals are generally based on Sun signs. It's also the easiest to identify because it is based only on your birthdate. The Sun is how we most often identify as the Self. It is often seen as the "male" or "father" energy in the chart. It's our being and our becoming, what our innate character is, and who we are learning to be in this lifetime. The Sun in your chart represents life, heart, vitality, essence, and consciousness.

The sign that your Sun is in is how you express your core identity—the part of you that shines in the world and acts. Think of the Sun itself—fiery, sometimes explosive, life-giving, and golden. How your Sun sign expresses itself is your light in the world. For example, in the sample chart, the Sun in Sagittarius will express itself most often as the freedom-seeking wanderer and wonderer but will also, at times, exhibit blind faith and moralistic tendencies. The aspects of the Sagittarius Sun sign you reflect is a free will choice.

While the Sun is obviously one of the most critical parts of the chart, it should not be viewed in isolation. The Sun is your core identity, but it is not the totality of who you are. It is always tempered by the other placements in the chart.

In the sample chart, the Sagittarius Sun has an Aquarius Ascendant, meaning that this freedom seeker also comes across as being unique and as one who thinks differently. This person also has a Libra Moon, which gives an emotional attachment to harmony and peace. You would also look at the mix of elements in the chart. The Sun sign (which is a Fire sign), the Ascendant (which is an Air sign), and the Libra Moon would make this person a thinker and always on the move, as the air fans the flames of the fire. The Sagittarius Sun in the tenth house suggests this person enjoys being out in the world. A natural leader, they are also very career-oriented.

Awareness of these placements might make it easier for the person to understand their need for freedom and intellectual stimulation, and this would lead to acceptance that they are not suited to any work or experiences that are repetitive and without mental stimulation.

A deep understanding and acceptance of your Sun sign helps you understand how your ego shows up in the world. It is, however, through this understanding of the sign and house that your Sun is in that you begin to have a greater awareness of your choices. There might be times that it is appropriate to your needs to embody one quality slightly more than the other. The constructs of positive and negative are not always set in stone, so try not to consider those black-and-white terms as you deepen your knowledge.

THE MOON

In the chart, the Moon is your emotional body. It's a reflective and receptive energy that responds and reacts. The Moon is your instinctive and intuitive self and how you unconsciously respond to the world around you. Whereas the Sun is your ego and the part of you that shines in the world and acts, the Moon is your soul, your most private yet most connected, reactive self.

The Moon is very much a feminine energy that acts in all of us. She is the Mother, your female ancestors, your home, and how you see all these things. She represents where you are coming from, your upbringing, and how you felt and feel about the world around you. Her silvery glow corresponds to the reflective, mirror like energy that is within you, and the face known as the "man in the moon" shows her very human side, the side that is the most immediately felt energy in the cosmos.

As children we are emotional beings; it is only as we develop that society teaches us that being "too emotional" or "too reactive" are undesirable qualities. Yet we are emotional beings at the core of our soul. What would it be like to allow more of that? To allow ourselves to feel to the full extent of our being. This, in part, is what this article aims to teach—how you can reach a point of deep acceptance in the way you operate emotionally, spiritually, and physically while learning to take the higher road in all aspects of your chart. A deep understanding and acceptance of the sign and house placement and aspects of your Moon help you understand how you respond and react to external stimuli in the world.

When you reach that point of deep acceptance and understanding, you can choose which path you take with awareness. For example, the Moon rules Cancer. Is your Moon in Cancer? If so, you would understand that this placement makes you more emotionally sensitive than some other signs and more receptive to other people's feelings. Moon in Cancer folk are also more inclined to be deeply nurturing and family oriented. None of these traits are good or bad; they just are. But once you accept that they just are, your awareness helps you deal with the deep sensitivity rather than perceiving it as "wrong." Viewing astrology in this way is all about making choices with awareness based on the embodiment of your energies. In this specific example, you can choose whether to have a good cry under the bedcovers or whether to treat yourself to a gentle healing massage if you are feeling emotionally hurt. Neither choice is wrong, but one might feel like the healthier response to you.

In the sample chart, the Moon is in Libra, which suggests this person likes a beautiful, harmonious, and airy home. This person is a diplomat; they can see two sides in every story and can compromise in almost every situation. This can, however, also lead to smoothing things over when it might be better off to discuss them, as Libra Moons dislike.

The Ascendant

Ascendant in Aries or Aries Rising

You probably have a sturdy, muscular frame with a lively, energetic face. You make intense and direct eye contact with others and may well have been told off for staring at people as a child because of this. You are probably of medium height and can show amazing feats of strength when necessary. Red hair is familiar with those with Aries on the Ascendant.

Always in a hurry, this can lead to your being accident-prone, especially with injuries to the head or face. A hasty temper turned inwards produces headaches or even migraines. Sporting activities or any form of physical exercise is an excellent release for this.

You meet life straightforwardly and energetically. You want to have control over your life, and a feeling of lack of control will manifest itself as illness. You often express yourself through dramatic outbursts, many times in anger or even other forms of self-destructive behavior.

Ascendant in Taurus or Taurus Rising

Taurus is the sign of the bull, and this may reflect in your body shape. Your well-shaped body displays a warm attractiveness and ripeness. In your later years, you may need to watch the tendency to gain weight too quickly. Your strong broad shoulders support either a long slender neck, or else you have an enormous neck size. Your most outstanding feature is your eyes and your gentle smile and voice. You may be bigboned. You enjoy dressing well, preferring soft colors.

You need to have your feet planted firmly on the ground while you aim for the stars, because you like to be able to see concrete results for your efforts. However high you aim, you like to remain in contact with the earthy and material side of life. This can have its drawbacks in as much as you have a tendency to hang on to people, things and experiences out of habit and a feeling of security, when there is no longer any need to. You need to learn to distinguish between when it is necessary to hang on, and when you should let go. When you head towards your goals you like to have plans and a structure to systematically work around.

You may need to consciously develop better habits with looking after your body and its requirements.

Ascendant in Gemini or Gemini Rising

You are the most youthful-looking of the zodiac with veritable Peter Pan looks. You may have neat, sharp facial features and a wiry frame. You can wear bright colors, mix patterns and fabrics and may love bizarre jewelry. You are lithe and agile with slender hands. Some people may think that you can look like two different people at different times.

Your ability to communicate, in fact your need to communicate, contributes to your sense of identity. You are extremely observant and can follow two or more conversations at once. You are a fast talker and may use your hands a lot. In any case, you always seem to have a lot to say. You are an excellent mimic and may also have a flair for languages.

You love to find out how people and things work and are quite clever at taking things apart and putting them back together again. Your curiosity makes you versatile and adaptable, but you may suffer from an over-abundance of diverse interests. In any case, you dislike being committed to only one thing, because you hate to lose alternatives.

Your abundance of nervous energy means that you are always on the move. You may appear highly strung. You are often in two minds about the situations that you are involved in.

Ascendant in Cancer or Cancer Rising

Your face is rounded with beautiful round, sensitive eyes that show concern and innocence. Your whole appearance speaks of softness and tenderness. You may not be that energetic, and you need to watch weight gain later in life. Fluid retention can also be a problem. As a female, you may be quite big-breasted. As a male, you may have quite a broad and fleshy chest in comparison with the rest of your body, especially your hips. You don't dress for glamour or to impress, instead you tend to prefer your old comfortable clothes rather than following uncomfortable fashion styles.

Growth in self-awareness comes to you through fully acknowledging, experiencing and respecting your true feelings, and developing the nurturing and caring side to your personality. You may feel overwhelmed at times by the depth of emotion that you feel. It is difficult for you to simply let go of a strongly felt emotion, unless you have another feeling just as powerful to take its place.

It is very healthy for you to play the mothering role, whether to a group of people, in the context of a business, or by nurturing a strongly felt cause. On the other hand, if you shun the role of nurturer, you will aim to find someone else to mother you. You will constantly be looking for the ideal mother type. There is also the possibility that you over-identify with your mother and find it hard to break away from the family unit.

You tend to approach issues and situations from a sideways angle and in a non-confrontational manner rather than head-on.

Ascendant in Leo or Leo Rising

You have great presence with a strong-featured face and a sunny glow of inner self-confidence. You display a regal quality in your posture and carriage, holding your head proudly, back straight, walking slowly and deliberately. You are probably well-built and taller than average. You have an eye for design and glamour. You are comfortable wearing strong colors and patterns. You may be quite vain about your hair.

You tend to feel that anything is better than being ordinary. You are preoccupied with emerging as an individual in your own right, and to do this you need to develop your sense of power and authority and exercise your creative expression.

Ascendant in Virgo or Virgo Rising

With Virgo on the Ascendant your body is probably neat and wiry, and you tend to use neat and economical movements. Your well-groomed appearance is mirrored in your cool and classic way of dressing, good posture, fine bone structure and animated expression. Physically, you possess good stamina. You tend to look younger than you are, all the way through into your later years.

In creating and defining yourself, you use self-criticism, mental analysis and discrimination, focusing on very specific points of your personality. You need to settle the practical management of the everyday necessities of daily life before you embarks on your grander aims in life.

You are very conscious of making sure that your body functions smoothly and well. You are very good at analyzing yourself and life in general. Still, you need to develop the ability to eject anything destructive to yourself. The danger exists that too much analysis can box you in to an existence that is overly rigid and tight. If you over-emphasize and become obsessive about order, correctness and precision, you may lose touch with your spontaneity and natural sense of flow.

Ascendant in Libra or Libra Rising

You are extremely attractive and have a warm and charming nature. Your features are usually refined, your bones delicate and your skin fair. Your movements are very graceful. You are aware of your attractiveness, but be careful that you don't fall into the trap of being vain and judging others by how beautiful they may look.

You are indecisive and tend to always sit on the fence. This is because you can always see the other's viewpoint. You are able see the viewpoint of everybody else around you. You must learn to force yourself to make choices and be prepared to take the consequences. Don't take the easy option of letting others decide for you. You can objectively and fairly assess any situation.

Ascendant in Scorpio or Scorpio Rising

You most likely have dark, brooding looks with thick, abundant hair and strongly marked eyebrows that frame the most important feature of your face, your eyes. Your eyes have a piercing, penetrating quality, so much so that many people are unable to meet the directness of your gaze. Overall, you give the impression of quietly contained power. Your movements are controlled, and your clothes are chosen for their dramatic value. With your commanding personality, you can instill fear and apprehension if you wish. There is an air of mystery about you, as well as veiled but potent sexuality.

Ascendant in Sagittarius or Sagittarius Rising

The Ascendant reveals how you present yourself to the outside world and the style in which you meet new experiences and life in general. When people first meet you, they meet your Ascendant rather than your Sun sign. The Ascendant may also indicate your physical characteristics.

Although you may not be tall, your legs are probably long and rangy. As a child, you may have been quite clumsy. Your long legs give you a bold way of walking, which you exercise, restlessly pacing up and down when you need to think. Your most outstanding feature is your wide brilliant smile, shining out of your open face. Although you prefer dressing casually most times, when you do dress up, you can look stunning.

Ascendant in Capricorn or Capricorn Rising

Your bone structure is distinctive, and you probably have good teeth. Your shoulders may be rounded, and physically you tend towards a wiry and lean frame. There may even be a certain devilish look to your face. Just as your life improves after the age of roughly forty, so do your looks lighten up, and you seem younger and more frivolous than years earlier. As a child, you looked serious and old for your years, but as you grow older, you seem to grow younger and better looking. You feel better and happier with every passing year.

Ascendant in Aquarius or Aquarius Rising

You are most likely tall and slim with good bone structure and clear, open and refined features. Your eyes are extraordinary, helping to give you an electric or magnetic aura. Your distinguishing feature is your hair, or if you are male, your beard perhaps. Your dress sense can add to your sometimes bizarre appearance, but even more conservatively dressed, you are always arresting. You tend to prefer bright electric colors over the more conservative and quiet shades.

Ascendant in Pisces or Pisces Rising

Your beautiful eyes are one of your most attractive features. Your complexion has a translucent quality, very pale if you are fair-skinned, or ripe and lush if you are dark-skinned. The clothes that you choose don't call attention to you, and they are soft and comfortable rather than fashionably gimmicky. Your feet tend to be large and your hair hard to manage.

Tarot the History

As a beginner in the art of tarot reading, for you to fully appreciate the beauty of Tarot, and for you to properly understand its global cultural significance, you need to be at least slightly familiar with its history.

The origin of the tarot deck and the art of tarot reading is shrouded in mystery and not fully understood. Since tarot reading is such an old art which has been in existence for at least half a millennium, it's easy to see why there would be different accounts about its actual place of birth, and its original inventor.

While the fact that a unanimous agreement on the origin of tarot may never be reached may be a tad frustrating for some tarot enthusiasts, the fact that its origin is mysterious, to say the least adds to the intrigue of the art, making it even more breathtaking and scintillating to learn. So, as you go through the pages and learn about the ancient art of Tarot reading, have it at the back of your mind that you are undergoing a process millions of people have been undergoing for over 500 years. Now, how is that for being a part of history?

According to records from European museums, tarot decks have been in existence since the 15th century, as evidenced in the tarot decks available in the museums' collections. These decks are nothing like modern tarot cards; they are sophisticated and highly elaborate – they are simply miniature works of art dripping with gold, probably made for the pleasure of royalties at the time.

According to some accounts from Egyptian mythology, tarot cards were created by the Egyptian god, Thoth. Thoth was said to have gifted the art of tarot reading to man from the great Egyptian pyramids to serve as a source of guidance and light for his subjects, and to enable them to find direction when they felt lost. It is speculated that somehow, the culture of reading Tarot cards may have died down among the Egyptian population, only for it to surface in Europe in the 18th century, courtesy of the Gypsies in their fancy caravans. They were an exotic sight to behold in ancient Europe.

When the Gypsies came to Europe with their simple yet fancy cultural inclinations, they quickly infiltrated the very fabric of the European society. Soon they were found in a lot of major European cities, especially in France. These Gypsies did Tarot readings for people in a similar fashion to the astrologers who read people's palms at carnivals and quaint little roadside shops today. In return for their services, the Gypsies collected silver pieces they used for day-to-day living, The Gypsies were extremely simple. Yet, incredibly profound people who discovered the secret to happiness was not accumulating wealth and rooting yourself to a point, it was in putting smiles on people's faces, while moving from city to city to find more faces to put smiles on. They didn't have a lot, but they had enough to leave an indelible imprint in the history.

Since Tarot reading encompassed the use of cards in divination and fortune-telling, several religious factions soon came out to condemn the practice of Tarot reading among the Gypsies, calling the Tarot cards 'the Devil's picture.' This notion is one that has been effectively passed down through several generations over the centuries, and one still held by some religious groups to date.

While everyone has the absolute prerogative to determine their own religious beliefs, it still feels pretty absurd that an art that has helped to define the way of life of a people (the Gypsies), and has helped to bring so many smiles to so many faces, create so many bonds, and even helped, in its little way to shape history as we know it is seen to be something evil.

If there is anything evil about Tarot, it would be its dangerous power to addict; once you start, there's no going back. You'll keep craving to know more, and the more you unleash your intuition, the more capable you will be of understanding the intricacies of life from different profound perspectives.

In all, it is important to note the aim of Tarot is not to corrupt your religious beliefs or make you practice voodoo. Not all. Tarot aims to help you find inner peace as you progress on your journey of life. Tarot aims to help you find a channel through which you can unleash your powerful intuition that the modern world has effectively helped you cage through the instilment of rigid rules and regulations right from your childhood. Tarot enlightens you and helps you to think outside the box. Tarot is all about harmony and flowing in sync with the universe – its basic principles are freedom and imagination.

The most reliable account of Tarot's history is it made its first appearance in Europe in the 15th century where the Tarot cards were used in a game called Tarrochi, an ancient form of the card game of bridge. This account is believable because the images used in the cards that made up the decks found in 15th century Europe are similar to the images etched onto the stained glass windows of European cathedrals and public buildings built around that period.

Even though Tarot cards were only played for fun at first, the possibility to use them in conjunction with a sharp intuition, an open mind, and perhaps some supernatural powers in fortunetelling soon led people to start using Tarot cards for divination purposes. Antione Court de Gebelin was one of the first public critics of Tarot reading – calling it an occultist practice only fit for heathens, despite the fact he also believed that some of the cards portrayed principles that formed the core of Christianity.

The first Tarot deck made specifically for divination was first made by a Parisian seed salesman known as Jean-Baptiste Alliete, who wrote under the pen name, Eteilla, which is simply his last name spelt backwards.

The beginning of the 20th century was a remarkable period in Tarot history. In 1909, Arthur E. Waite, a member of the Golden Dawn, a secret English magical society, published the first standardized deck of Tarot cards, and called it the R.W.S Tarot deck. The paintings on the cards were made by Pamela Colman Smith, and that Tarot deck is the most widely accepted and soled Tarot deck in the world till date.

Over the years, slight modifications have been made to improve user experiences. Still, the original Rider-Waite-Smith deck remains the foundation upon which all these developments have been made. In 1943, Aleister Crowley collaborated with the talented artist Frieda Harris to create the Thoth Tarot deck, the second most common Tarot deck model in the world.

In the earlier parts of the 20th century, fortune-telling Gypsies still used Tarot cards for divination. Even though the Gypsies have faded away with time, the practice of reading Tarot cards remains highly appreciated and widely practiced.

In the 1960s, important articles that helped the average man with no contact with Tarot to have comprehensive knowledge about the art were published, further exposing Tarot to different parts of the world. Eden Gray published 'The Tarot Revealed' and 'Mastering the Tarot', both in the 60s. Gray's teachings of tarot reading encompassed the interpretations used by fortune tellers to read the cards, and the practices of secret societies in ancient Europe in using the cards for divination. Other important Tarot articles that helped to lay the foundation for Tarot literature were '78 Degrees of Wisdom' by Rachel Pollock and 'Tarot for Yourself' by Mary. K. Greer.

Over the years, since its introduction, the basis upon which Tarot reading is built has shifted gradually from fortunetelling to psychology. In the first centuries of Tarot reading up till the beginning of the 20th century, the principle of Tarot reading existed on the most people's general belief in fortunetelling. Back in those days, people were open to idea of a supernatural force helping to reveal hidden information through the card readings. However, with time, has come the evolution of the society, and people no longer hold the kinds of beliefs in the supernatural that they used to. Therefore, for Tarot reading to survive as an art, its foundation; its basis had to undergo a paradigm shift from fortunetelling to psychology.

Currently, the principle of Tarot reading is based on a delicate psychological understanding by card readers and querents alike. People in the modern day understand that they have their freewill, no matter what the card readings are. However, they still believe that considering the results of a card reading with an open, intuitive mind would allow them to be able to find solutions to their problems from perspectives that could not be reached by mere analytical thinking. That notion is the current bedrock of Tarot reading among most modern adherents.

However, for any entity to truly thrive and survive through the ages, it must continue to evolve. The truth, however, is people have come to accept psychology FULLY as the basis for the existence of Tarot reading in the modern dispensation, thereby effectively blocking all routes through which tarot reading could further evolve in the future. The basis of tarot reading has evolved from being a type of fortunetelling to being a function of psychological beliefs – it has to keep evolving to keep growing.

Therefore, instead of just accepting psychology as the supreme basis for the functioning of Tarot reading, it would make a lot more sense instead, if we were more open-minded as adherents of this ancient art, to allow different thought patterns to run. People should be allowed to believe whatever they want, so that when the society evolves, tarot reading can evolve along with it.

Tarot Cards and their Meanings

The Major Arcana
Traditionally, the cards are numbered in Roman numerals from I to XXI (1 to 21), with the remaining card, The Fool, either left unnumbered or given a "0." The ordering of the cards is consistent across decks, except for the Justice and Strength cards (which will be explained below), and the position of the Fool, which is typically at the start of the sequence but can also be found at the end.

Various schools of interpretation for these cards have developed over time, with one approach often influencing another. However, the concept of the Major Arcana as representing a "journey" or "path" of some kind has been a recurring theme over the centuries.

In this framework, the cards may reflect the major events we encounter as we move through our physical lives, or they may represent our psychological or spiritual journey, as we experience the lessons our souls chose to learn during this present incarnation. In practice, the Major Arcana tends to address both physical and intangible aspects of our life experience.

There is no standard, universally accepted set of interpretations for the Major Arcana in the context of the Fool's Journey, but many guides and seasoned Tarot experts offer sufficiently similar meanings to create a consensus. As you familiarize yourself with the cards over time, you will no doubt come to your understanding of each one, and how it relates to you on your journey.

The Minor Arcana
While the cards in the Minor Arcana may seem less significant than the "trump" cards, they represent the essential ingredients that make up our lives, without which, the lessons of the Major Arcana would have no context.

Each suit of the Minor Arcana is centered on a particular realm of experience: ideas, feelings, action, and manifestation. As these cards make up the bulk of the deck, they tend to be more prevalent in a reading than the Major Arcana cards.

In modern decks, the suits are most often known as wands, cups, swords, and pentacles. Still, some decks keep to the more traditional medieval names and symbols, while others have adapted different names and symbols altogether. The more widely used alternate suit names are listed beneath each suit description.

Wands

The suit of Wands represents the realm of inspiration, intention, and ambition. When we are feeling creative, inspired, spurred to action, and envisioning outcomes we are utilizing Wand energy.

There is a distinction to be made here between thought and action, however. Action is not yet dominant at the Wands stage, and sometimes this suit can remind us that enthusiastic beginnings still require follow-through. Wands also represent risk-taking and initiative, as we desire to grow, create, and expand our horizons. Because we are essentially motivated by desire—either to manifest a positive outcome or avoid a negative one—feelings of both apprehension and excited anticipation are connected to the cards of this suit.

On the whole, Wands are considered positive cards, and often show up in a reading as a sign of encouragement.

Cups

The suit of Cups is the realm of emotion, creativity, psychic insights, love, empathy, and matters of the heart in general. The Cups tend to represent the feelings that accompany, or arise out of, the thoughts we are having about a given situation. These feelings tend to influence our behavior, whether or not we're consciously aware of them.

A full range of emotions—both pleasant and unpleasant—is present within this suit, so some cards may appear to be negative, depending on the reading. Yet any cards that assist with getting clarity on a situation should be appreciated.

Cups can also speak to the benefits and potential pitfalls of psychic gifts and empathy. While an open and conscious mind is generally an advantage, taking on other people's energy or getting overwhelmed by psychic impressions is not.

Swords

The suit of Swords represents the realm of action, movement, and struggle, as well as logic, reason, and intellect. The effort involved in pursuing a goal, which can often be perceived as struggle, is the realm of Sword energy. It can require much effort to turn our ideas into reality, but this is also where the most learning tends to occur.

Action is the result of the combining of ideas (Wands) with emotions (Cups). Yet, the Swords advise rationality and detachment from expectations of specific outcomes. Because of this, the cards of this suit can be perceived as cold or harsh with their messages, as they cut straight through any illusions we may be clinging to. In some cases, Swords may signify strength, authority, and power, as well as the more unfortunate elements of human nature that lead to violence and suffering.

The suit is not overwhelmingly unfavorable, but the Swords do tend to bring up the trickier aspects of a situation.

Pentacles

The suit of Pentacles is all about manifestation, results, groundedness, and material well-being. These cards often appear to issues of finances, abundance, business pursuits, and the home and family, as well as the physical body.

Pentacles represent the results of the initial inspiration (Wands), which is then responded to in the feeling realm (Cups), and consequently acted upon (Swords). While the other three suits predominantly inhabit the invisible realms of non-physical energy, Pentacles are concerned with the material, physical plane. However, they can also represent the feelings of security we all seek on the material plane, and the sense of being grounded in one's sovereignty as a person.

The cards of this suit are generally considered favorable, as they speak to the rewards of our efforts. Still, they can also reflect fear around not having (or being) enough.

The Significance of Numbers

As with many other forms of divination, numbers are highly significant in the Tarot. From the time of the modern deck's development in Marseilles, the number assigned to each card has been considered to be important to its meaning. In decks with non-illustrated pip cards, numerological correspondences are especially important to interpreting meaning. Each of these cards bears a number between 1 and 10—the number set at the core of numerology, also referred to as "the decade."

While different Tarot traditions may draw from one or more numerological systems (such as Pythagorean, Chaldean, or Kabbalistic numerology) when it comes to interpretation, the number descriptions below are representative of common themes and associations for each number in the decade. These core characteristics can help you get a clearer sense of how each numbered pip card is distinct from the others in its suit.

One is the beginning of that which is about to form or take shape. Represented by the Ace of each suit, it is considered to hold the "seed" or absolute potential of a situation. This potential may be dormant, and may even be unknown to you, just as a seed can be either intentionally planted or arrive unexpectedly on the wind. Either way, this potential needs further action and development for manifestation to take place, just as a single point in geometry needs another for a shape to take form.

Two is the necessary "next step" that allows the potential of the one to become something more. In geometry, where one point has nowhere to "go," two points make a line possible. In the Minor Arcana, these cards often depict two people. Still, this number can symbolize aspects of duality, polarity, balance, and choices as well as relationships.

Three represents the first fruition of the balanced union of the two. It is the synthesis of inspiration, cooperation and growth. Three points are the minimum required for the first closed shape—the triangle—to form. Three is also found three times (3, 6, 9) within the decade. It represents expression, creativity, manifestation, and integration. Three moves beyond partnership into group collaboration—beyond the balanced polarity of two into something more that requires a new, more complex balance—a pattern that will now begin to repeat through the rest of the numbers.

Four is some stability and completion. Added to the triangle of the three, it creates the first three-dimensional shape, the tetrahedron. In this sense the four is the manifestation of the initial idea of the one into material form. It represents balance, as seen in the four legs of a table, and secure foundations. Four is also associated with justice and fair dealings (as in the expression "fair and square"). Its metaphysical significance is seen in the four elements, the four cardinal directions, and the four seasons.

Five, like the three, is some outward expansion, coming along to disrupt the perfect symmetry of the four so that new manifestation can occur. The cycle of creation requires change, which is often disruptive and can cause uncertainty, difficulty and even chaos for periods. However, this imbalance spurs new movement, which opens up opportunities for new developments that could not arise otherwise.

Six brings order to the chaos of the five. Like the four, it is some balance and harmony, but since it integrates every stage of the one's manifestation thus far, its structure is more complex. As the first product of an odd and even number, it reconciles differences and restores equilibrium. Six represents successful adjustments to past challenges, and can often signify a victory. It represents the qualities of compassion and cooperation, responsibility, and service to others.

Seven is some strong mystical significance in spiritual traditions around the world. It is found in nature in the visible light spectrum, the planets visible from Earth, and the musical tones of the scale. We live in the rhythm of the seven through the days of the week. Seven creates a new dynamic out of the six by adding the one, creating new changes and opportunities. It represents choices, mystery, uncertainty, spirituality, wisdom, and the potential for perfection.

Eight brings back the energy of balance and symmetry, now as a double of the four. The continuous line of the eight resembles the symbol for infinity. There is stability on both the material and spiritual planes as circumstances harmonize with the cosmic order of the Universe. This brings new energy and power for accomplishing goals, organizing and integrating what has manifested so far, and bringing things nearer to completion. Eight represents progress, capability, regeneration, success, and personal power.

Nine is the final single digit, and as such symbolizes the end of a cycle, but in the numerological system of the decade, the completion is still to come. Nine appears in every multiple of itself in the form of adding the digits in the multiple, representing the patterns of perfection found throughout the Universe. It is the triple of the three, a mystical and powerful configuration. It represents affirmation, culmination, and the surety of success, as well as boundaries, limits, and strength.

Ten contains the properties of the one, but now on a new level. As the final number of the decade, it completes whatever was left unfinished or unresolved in the nine. It sets the stage for the next cycle of manifestation to occur. Ten represents wholeness, fulfillment, and reaping the benefits of persistent effort. It is some resolution, consolidation, and readiness for new beginnings.

Having a sense of the esoteric meanings of individual numbers can add enormous depth to your understanding of the cards, especially when it comes to non-illustrated pips. But if you don't have experience with numerology, don't worry—you can still access interpretations for all of the cards, either through this guide, your personal deck's guide, or other sources on the Tarot.

If you find that a certain number or pair of numbers keeps showing up in your readings, however, it's worth looking up their esoteric meanings, as this signifies that the Universe is trying to tell you something.

Numerology, what is it?

Known as the science of numbers, its etymological meaning came from the Latin word numerous, which means number and the Greek word logos that means a thought, idea, expression, or word. Numerology links numbers with events in one's life and surroundings. It is associated with astrology and other mystical and divine entities. It foretells a person's future by digging into one's potentiality and nature and other life's projections. It gives you a look into what your destiny is by considering the planets' movements in the sky, attributes, and methodology, as well as deities. This idea has not been recorded in any artifact until 1907. Its origin cannot be accurately determined but the earliest recorded history points to Egypt and Babylon approximately 10,000 years ago. It became popular among scholars in Greece who too are not certain as to this concept's origin.

In Philosophy

Along with other philosophers, Pythagoras, the Greek philosopher who postulated the famous Pythagorean theorem ( ), which states that the area of the square of the hypotenuse is equal to the sum of the squares of the two sides, believed in the greater certainty of numbers because of its practicality and ease in classifying or regulating them. He was known for his famous line, 'The world is built upon the power of numbers'. And numerology was based on this principle. According to the famous Christian theologian and writer, St. Augustine of Hippo, numbers serve as a confirmation of the truth that deities offer to humans. It has become their way of communication or better yet a universal language. He further explained the existence of numerical relationships with basically everything and it is just up to you to know these secrets or have them revealed by divine grace.

In Religion

As this was considered as one that deals with the paranormal side, magic, and other forms of divinations, which were also classified as among the civil violations in the Roman Empire during the reign of Constantine I, numerology was not approved by the Christian authority (council of Christian bishops) and was set aside during their convention. This happened in 325 AD.

Notwithstanding the abolition of the belief, it cannot be denied that its religious significance remained alive. As analyzed by Dorotheus of Gaza, the Jesus number was still used especially among conservative Greek Orthodox circles. Religious architecture and the Bible admit of numerology. In the bible, the number 3 and 7 are among the favorites. The number 7 was usually the number for which a famine would last. More often, 7 is followed by 8, which signified change. To cite an example, Ahab was sent 7 times by his Master Elijah to Mt. Carmel to look for a certain cloud, which he was able to find only on the 8th time. Here is another example: 7 days was required of Miriam to spend in the wilderness after they (Miriam and Aaron) spoke ill of Moses' marriage with an Ethiopian woman. She then joined Exodus on the 8th day.

In religious architecture, the evidence of numerological influences can be seen in Chartres Cathedral that is the number 306.

In Alchemy

Related to numerology are some alchemical theories. Jabir ibn Hayyan, a Persian alchemist had his experiments founded on the names of substances found in the Arabic language.

In Literature

The Garden of Cyrus which is a literary discourse written by Sir Thomas Browne in 1658 embodied the concept of numerology throughout art designs and nature with the use of the quincunx pattern, a 5-point geometric pattern with 4 of its points forming a rectangle or square and the 5th is found at the center.

As an ancient system of learning information about your life and future with numbers, numerology is a useful tool that will help a person gain knowledge and wisdom about one's life story. It is practically one of the oldest self-help tools available to us since it originated back to the years of ancient civilizations.

You may ask, is numerology pure mathematics? No. It is a science of numbers and the math involved is very basic and simple. Even elementary graders would not have any problems calculating for the core numbers that will be mentioned in this article! How wicked is that? And even as we mention math when we talk about numerology, at the end of the day, it is all about characteristics and personality traits that make up a person and how these elements combine to define who we are right now and who we will be in the future. It talks about the way we are characterized and it reveals our most probable goals in life.

Before we get started, let us first look into a couple of things that would deepen your understanding about numerology.

1. Numerology can help you uncover your life's path and purpose. Those reading this article may be doing so for various reasons. However, I bet that they all have something to do with

your life. Are you having trouble with your career? Are you searching for love? Do you wish to have good health? Are you uncertain about what to do with your life? Those questions are probably just some of what is lurking in your thoughts and you wondered if numerology could help you answer them. Fortunately, for you, numerology can!

2. Numerology is not a new fad. Even though some of you may just have heard of numerology, its roots can be traced back allegedly to the time of Pythagoras, a Greek mathematician and mystic, around 2, 500 years ago. However, rumor has it that even though Pythagoras may be deemed as the father of modern numerology, the Chaldeans of ancient Babylon can be credited with developing a system of numerology even before Pythagoras' time.

3. There are various systems of numerology. Aside from the Western system of numerology that we are going to utilize, there exists other forms of numerology including Chaldean, Chinese, Indian, and Kabbalistic.

4. It rests on the premise that the whole universe and our lives is a system and there is order to this system. Numerologists claim that the whole universe and its elements are part of a system and systems can be broken down to the basest elements, which are numbers. Basing from the argument that the universe – and with it, the stars, galaxies, constellations, etc. – can be understood, it must also be assumed that life and people's personalities can be figured out as well since we are a part of the whole universe.

5. In numerology, numbers mean the same thing wherever it may appear. It does not matter which system of numerology you use, once you get the grasp of the meaning of each number, gaining wisdom from it is very easy.

6. Lessons and challenges are just some of the facets of wisdom that you will procure from numerology. Since numerology rests on the premise that we are on the eternal search for growth and self-mastery, numbers will present us lessons that we can mature from and obstacles that we would need to overcome. Also, these same numbers will help us break through these obstacles to fulfill our destinies, as there are certain sets of suggested life lessons that we need to acknowledge and embrace.

7. Numbers represent both positives and negatives. Since life does not offer us just good things or just bad things, numbers will hold both sources of happiness and display challenges. Not only that, they will also reveal your strengths and weaknesses. So get ready to be slapped in the face with your faults. Nevertheless, these revelations are not something you should veer away from because it will make you more self-aware and it can be the platform that you can use to improve yourself.

8. Names and birthdates are vital to numerology. Numerology believes that our names and birthdates can show a comprehensive amount of who we are. This is because both of them reflect our depth and discloses our internal traits and thoughts. How is this so? Numerologists claim that naming a child is so intuitive. There is a reason why a couple named their child Anna even though they may not be privy to the exact reason. There is no randomness when it neither comes to naming a child nor is there in the date of her birth.

How to Calculate your Numerology and What it Means?

Pythagoras developed Pythagorean numerology before the time of Christ in ancient Greece. Pythagoras believed that numbers could be used to explain all things in the universe. He used mathematics for spiritual matters. This method of numerology is often referred to as modern numerology because it is the most recently developed method, and it has come to be the method most widely used in modern times, particularly in the Western world. Popular legend states that Pythagoras used the practice of numerology to use name-changing as a way to alter the destiny of an individual, predict what events would take place at certain locations, and determine the future fates of individuals. In this system, the letters of the alphabet are assigned a corresponding number based on their position in the alphabet. Both the date of birth and the name are used in Pythagorean Numerology, and the relationships between the two are studied.

This method uses the full name that is given at birth because that is the name that will determine an individual's numerical makeup. The birth name will tell what impression a person is most likely to make on other people, what the person naturally expresses the best, and what motivates a person, mentally and psychologically. The other most important number in Pythagorean numerology is the actual date of birth, which is used to determine the number of the life path of the individual.

Those who subscribed to the Pythagorean method of numerology were not simply interested in applying the science of numbers to determining the individual strengths and weaknesses of people. They believed that numbers were present in vast quantities in the natural world and that most things in life were ruled by a series of numbers. They firmly believed that numbers possessed mystical abilities and properties and the "all is number" meaning that anything in the world can be described in terms of proportions and numbers and everything in the world can be measured. This belief is the basic foundation of the practice of numerology.

Every letter in the alphabet has a numeric value, and every number has its related cosmic vibration. When the letters in a person's name and the date on which the person was born are combined in a particular formula, this will give an insight into how the vibrations are related to each other. This formula will give information to the person's purpose in life as a part of the overall plan of the cosmos. It will also reveal details of a person's motivations, natural talents, weaknesses, strengths, and character tendencies. Numerology is one of the best tools in use today that will help an individual develop a better insight into their overall physiological and cosmic makeup.

The soul's number, or the heart's desire number, is the element that is at the core of a person's numerology chart. It is used to open up the numerology chart and remove the layers covering it. The soul number is responsible for unlocking the person that is kept hidden from the outside world—the spiritual and eternal person deep inside, the more intense and deeper person. When this personal code is opened and deciphered to reach its true meaning, then the true meaning of the person is made available to the outside world, what motivates the person on a spiritual level, the fears and passions, the urges and inner cravings, and the desires that are hidden deep in the core of the person. The guiding force behind exactly what the soul is expecting to experience on earth is the soul urge.

Life often begins once this number is revealed. The person's life begins to finally make sense as anxiety and depression begin to drift away. The soul can finally find meaning in the world, given the energy it needs to thrive and the ability to be nurtured and recognized. Using the methods of Pythagorean numerology, the number for the soul urge is determined by using only the vowels of the full name. The reason for this is that consonants are said with a sharp edge to them, and they have a definite end and a definite beginning. Consonants are considered to be the containers for the way people express themselves and for the traits that people reveal to the outside world, and consonants represent a person's public personality. Vowels are made from the timeless and formless essence inside of a person and formed from spirit and air. They are pronounced with a breath that flows freely.

Remove all of the consonants in the full name. Determine the values that are assigned to each letter and then add all of the numbers together. Keep adding and reducing until there is just one single digit. This is an example of determining a soul number:

A = 1, E = 5, I = 9, O = 6, U = 3, Y = 7

Mary Anne Smith

A + Y + A + E + I = 1+ 7+ 1+5+9 = 23 = 2+3 = 5

Mary Anne Smith's soul urge number is 5

"Y" is sometimes a vowel and sometimes a consonant. It is used as a vowel when it is the only sound in the syllable, like in the names Kylie or Terry. It is also used as a vowel when it comes before a vowel that is in the next syllable, and it makes a vowel sound, as in the names Mya or Hyacinth. The letter "Y" is considered to be a consonant when it is used to make the hard sound of a consonant like in the names Yulee or Yoda or when it comes after a vowel in the same syllable and does not make a vowel sound that is separate from the other vowel sound, like Maya or Grayson.

When all of the numbers are added together and condensed to the lowest possible number, that number is called the Master Number. When the numbers are being added together and a total of eleven or twenty-two is reached, that is where the adding stops. These are also considered to be Master Numbers. Once the soul number has been determined, the interpretation can be determined.

The Significance of Names

Analyzing a person's name using numerology is a way to provide them with knowledge about themselves by interpreting the energy that is represented by that person's name. The analysis can give a considerable amount of personal understanding when it is appropriately and accurately interpreted.

In focusing only on the name part of the analysis, the person's birth date is omitted, and the name is used. This will allow the name analysis to be clearer and deeper than a general numerology reading. When a name analysis is done, three name numbers are specifically analyzed. These three important name numbers are the personality number, the soul's urge or heart's desire number, and the destiny number.

The destiny number is determined from all of the letters in the person's full name given at birth. The soul's urge or heart's desire number is derived from all the vowels in the person's full birth name. And the personality number comes from the consonants in the person's full birth name. The destiny number is the number that tells how a person will live their life. The soul's urge number shows the person's real motivations and desires. The personality number will show the person how other people see them.

Number One – Number one people are all about moving forward. The number one person has leadership capabilities, independent nature, and the spirit of a pioneer. Sometimes, ones are boastful or bossy because they are using an inflated sense of self-importance to hide insecurities. Ones need to be careful not to become too lonely by always wanting to be first. Number ones still need to have the support of lovers, family, and friends.

Number Two – Two is aligned with harmony, balance, and sensitivity. Two takes on the position of the mediator in life, bringing together combating forces to create harmony by using kindness, empathy, and compassion. Twos have intuition and psychic abilities. Twos can sometimes feel unacknowledged or underappreciated because they are so sensitive. They need to realize that true validation lies within themselves and not look for it externally.

Number Three – The number three is the very essence of creation. It is two forces joined together to communicate. These people are gifted communicators who easily share concepts that are pioneering and innovative by using speaking, writing, and art. They love to make other people happy and their work uplifts, motivates, and inspires other people. But the number three person might withdraw from other people entirely because they feel misunderstood. Their imaginations tend to be overactive, so it is good for them to enjoy quiet times to recharge, restore, and reset.

Number Four – Four is a firm believer in the physical world and in building a legacy that lasts through a strong physical structure. Their energy is involved with strengthening their roots. They desire to support growth by creating logical systems by being responsible, hardworking, and practical. These people need to remember that rules were made to enhance situations and not to inhibit growth because the number four can quickly become rigid. Fours should take a few risks and try to think outside of the box to feel more inspired and liberated.

Number Five – Five is defined by the freedom that this progressive, adventurous, and free-thinking number enjoys. A number five will use all of their senses to explore the greater world. These people are known for their vivacious, impulsive, and playful spirit. Fives can become bored by the daily routine because they are always seeking excitement, and this can include personal and professional commitments.

Number Six – A number six person has an empathic, supportive, and nurturing nature. They can solve problems that are either physical or emotional. They help others with a gentle yet straightforward approach. They can communicate easily with animals or children. However, these people want to parent everyone and everything they come into contact with, and they need to learn that not every creature on earth needs a parent. They need to realize that all creatures need to follow their path.

Number Seven – These people are known for their analytical skills and their investigative abilities. A detail-oriented individual, they are also driven by strong inner wisdom. They have an inventive and humorous spirit and a keen eye for the flaws in any system. They tend to be perfectionists.

Number Eight – This number is aligned with financial success and material wealth. Their natural magnetism allows them to take charge easily in any situation because they are goal-oriented and ambitious. These people can easily become workaholics and can be excessively possessive and controlling. Eights will realize that the greater good lies in helping others and giving back to the world at large.

Number Nine – Number nines are old souls. These people can use incoming information to create a whole out of many little pieces. Nines want to reach an elevated level of consciousness and to help other people reach it too. These people are not afraid to change, but they must remember to keep themselves well-grounded in reality.

Master Number Eleven – This number has the energy of the number two. It uses it to heal other people with its high level of psychic abilities. Elevens often develop extrasensory talents because of extreme life events they have lived through. This number is aligned with philosophical balance, awareness, and spiritual enlightenment.

Master Number Twenty-Two – This number is often referred to as the Master Builder, and it expands on the energies of the number four. These people are inspired to transcend immediate realities by creating platforms within the physical realm. They like to join the powers of the intangible and the tangible. They are always looking for something to change and are dependable, creative, and diligent.

Fibonacci Numbers

The finding of Fibonacci numbers in human physiology as well as many other places in nature, is likewise not trivial. By denying their significance, I think we miss the point of their existence. Nature accomplishes things by logical extension. If such extension results in certain kinds of mathematic relationships like pi, the Fibonacci series, or any other mathematic relationships, then so be it. We must then look beneath these phenomena for the process that gives rise to these properties.

We see quartz crystals or snowflakes growing in their characteristic way related to the bond angles of the molecules from which they are formed. Are similar chemical patterns represented in biologic individuals, and does biologic evolution simply follow these kinds of biochemical templates? This question, first posed by Stuart Kaufman, may only find an answer in quantum mechanics itself—the field of physics related to particles and atoms.

Mario Livio has another perspective on this subject. In his article, The Golden Ratio—the Story of Phi, he states: "Physical systems usually settle into states that minimize the energy. The suggestions is therefore that phyllotaxis simply represents a state of minimal energy..." Fibonacci numbers may occur in biologic life because they represent the least energy, and the most order, of a biologic entity.

To deepen our inquiry about how phyllotaxis and Fibonacci numbers found their way into life's architecture, we must ask whether these patterns of organization are present even in particles and atoms: Are biologic forms simply copying more inorganic ones? Perhaps the only real solution lies hidden in the original patterns of organization laid down at the beginning of everything, before there was life, or chemicals, or even atoms; A time when the universe was just a sea of energy emerging from some great causative event.

Is this where everything in nature learned mathematics? Did evolution learn the art that we see expressed in physical and biologic structures, of building complex forms from simpler ones from an initial set of conditions present at the start of the universe? If so, what were those initial conditions? More questions, profoundly unanswered, are encountered in our search for the highest brain mechanism and the roots of consciousness.

Fibonacci Series

The Fibonacci series has been discovered in many natural processes, curiously dominating the framework of the human body. Could such a framework similarly be used to create musical scales? To this end, we again consider its numbers: 0,0,1,2,3,5,8,13,21...where each successive number in the series is formed by adding the two numbers that immediately precede it. This recursive series forms ratios, angles, and structural relationships between the adjacent elements of the series. The ratio is called the Golden Mean .6189339887....) also called Phi;) and its formulations is found below: The Golden Angle is 137.5 degrees (Phi times 360 degrees= 225. .5 degrees,. 360 minus 225.5 = 137.5.

When fractions are made from adjacent numbers of the Fibonacci series, they form slightly differing ratios from the beginning numbers of the series to the higher ones. The ratio between 0 and 1 (0 / 1) is zero, and the ratio between 1 and 0 (1 / 0) is a calculation that, though being virtually banned from our mathematics, still closes on infinity. The first two numbers of the series, 0 and 0, form ratios that we don't like to think about.

But from this point on, things get a little better. The numbers 1 and 2 form ratios of 1/2 and 2/1, both somewhat more respectable. If one were to multiply a note like C (frequency +261.63 cps), one gets nothing but octaves traveling up and down the keyboard from this calculation. C (261.63) times 1/2 creates descending octaves of C, and C (261.63) times 2 creates ascending octaves of C. There is a wave function—a mathematic equation describing the properties of how waves behave. There is also one of how various scale tones of a musical system interact.

The next two numbers in the series, 2 and 3, form ratios of 2/3 and 3/2. When these ratios are multiplied by C(261.63), two twelve-tone scales are formed in either direction that when modified to fit within a single octave and scale tone averages compensated for, form a Fibonacci twelve-tone scale that is quite similar to what we know of as the logarithmic tempered scale. This fourth-order Fibonacci scale, with (0:1/ 1:0, !:1/ 1:1, 1:2/ 2:1)being the first, second, and third order scales, is found below in the following diagram and its variances to the tempered twelve-tone scale noted in scale tunings deviations.

The Fibonacci series doesn't stop at 3, but keeps on going out to infinity. In successive orders of Fibonacci scales, having ratios 3/5: 5/3: and 5/8: 8/5, strange things start occurring. The number of tones that can be fit into the octave rapidly expands from 12 (in the 2/3:3/2 fourth-order scale) to 19 notes in a fifth-order scale (3:5/5:3), and to 28 notes in a sixth-order scale (5:8/8:5). But these Fibonacci scales don't keep increasing in the number of notes they generate endlessly, for in the higher order scales, the number of notes begins to diminish again. The Fibonacci ratios of these scales gradually wavers closer and closer to the calculated value of Phi, and the note counts of these scales finally settles down into an odd kind of scale having thirteen notes. These scale variations are described in the next few series of diagrams.

The Fibonacci scales don't exactly represent either strictly linear or logarithmic principles. They seem to range over a wide area of tonal landscapes, happily generating relationships between tonal intervals that we are familiar with, and some that we definitely are not. When we can corral these intervals into a single octave, they can be compared to the linear and logarithmic scales we have noted. But the Fibonacci scales are neither, for in their elaboration they span many octaves, and are best represented as a spiral of tones rather than as ladders. What really emerges from these scales are self-similar curvatures of a helical nature that travel in ascending and descending directions.

Lastly, ratios of the Fibonacci series gradually settle down into a single number: The Golden Mean. Phi.

Higher-order Fibonacci Scales

The above higher-order Fibonacci scale helixes approximate Phi (1.6180339887498948482045868343 65..., and it's reciprocal: 0.6180339887498948482045868343 65 ...) as they turn and spin their way through octaves of 4ths and 5ths. As we noted, these ratios generate recursive numbers that can be represented graphically as spirals, one of the primary patterns of Fibonacci numbers found in plants. These spirals, arising from any fundamental frequency, generate the same tonal series in either the ascending or descending direction they travel, enhancing, if nothing else, the amplitude of these tonal elements. In other words, tonal series based on the various orders of the Fibonacci scale, represent enhanced nodes of energy amplitudes. Such enhancements, seen only partially represented in other scale systems, such as the enharmonic scale, favor octaves, and less so other tonal combinations. Fibonacci scales represent the summation of scale-tone amplitudes that entrain the scale fundamental into an overarching logical system applicable not just to music, but to all vibrating energies. There is a wave function—a mathematic equation describing the properties of how waves behave, and there is one of how various scale tones of a musical system interact.

The underlying basis of harmony is founded not on what one tone may sound like in relation to some other tone, but on how all tones are related to an overall coherent system of tones: Coherent, a word defined most often as understandable, but yet having another meaning in energetic mechanisms. Coherent light such as emitted by a laser, is very ordered, and doesn't scatter because it is in phase. Their wave peaks and valleys are synchronistic.

Fibonacci scales describe this logic in music, and if this is a correct analysis, then these numbers describe the harmonic logic of energy in general. This logic is neither linear nor strictly logarithmic, but helical, and based on naturally occurring amplitudes of nodal energies present in any dynamic energy system.

For example, a musical scale based on middle C, having a fundamental frequency of 261.63 cps, multiplied by the above number and it's reciprocal (Phi), has no appreciable differentials in the ascending and descending scale intervals it generates. Both calculations wind up exactly on an octave of C and form a thirteen tonal scale. When we compare the intervals of this scale to the tempered scale, an interesting thing happens. There develops a kind of 'curvature" in the tonal relationships of this highest-order Fibonacci scale that, when compared with the tempered scale, has some 'wild-card' notes around the mid-scale region of F, F#, and Gas noted diagrams. These notes, in modern music, are sometimes called 'blue notes' because they are favorites in jazz and blues improvisations.

The significance of this ultimate termination of Fibonacci series and its associated thirteen-note musical scale is a quandary to I think has significance in the patterns they form, and add this scale to the overall puzzle of how Fibonacci numbers in general are written into the structures of nature.

What is Enneagram– Harmony Triads and Nine Types

Understanding personality is the key to understanding, not just other people, but ourselves as well. At times, we can be shocked by our behavior, unsure where the actions we've taken have come from. It is through becoming fully knowledgeable about our personality, are we able to fully grow. This is where the Enneagram of Personality comes in.

The Enneagram of Personality, or rather just Enneagram, has been taking the world by storm for the last quarter of a century, and yet, some are skeptical about it. They may have good reasons, but without the knowledge of what it is, it can become rather frightening.

Enneagram is derived from the Greek word ennea, which means "nine" and gramma, which means "written" or "drawn." It is called so since it is a personality test that takes into consideration nine different personality types. The exact origins of the enneagram are under dispute; however, the contemporary enneagram, the one that we see today, is said to have started in 1915 with various men and thinkers who had taken their part in making it what it is today.

Personality Types

The Enneagram is a diagram of nine separate personality types with each individual being born into one of those types dominating over all the others, something that comes out in childhood. This means that an individual does not change from one type to another for any reason, but rather, this is something that has a genetic predisposition.

The Reformer

The first personality type on the Enneagram diagram is called the Reformer. In some instances, it is also called the perfectionist as individuals that have this as their primary personality type work towards becoming idealistic with a very strong sense of right and wrong. These individuals pride themselves on being responsible, honest, and having common sense, getting annoyed with individuals who do not take life as seriously as they do.

This personality is characterized by the individual having a sense of a mission that they need to accomplish, which most of the time leads them to improve on the world around them. Throughout history, these are the individuals that have left what seemed to be perfect and comfortable lives in order to accomplish a greater goal, such as Joan of Arc or Gandhi.

The Helper

Second, on the Enneagram personality diagram is The Helper, and their sole motivator is to feel loved. They are known as being caring and helpful. Individuals with this personality type are the most genuinely helpful, and if they find themselves less than fortunate health-wise, they still try to see themselves as the most helpful.

They work on being the most helpful in order to fulfill their need for acceptance, but also because it sincerely warms their hearts. Helpers consider themselves to be the richest when they've been able to be generous towards other people, which makes people gravitate towards them. This provides them with the need for the closeness of friendship and family.

On the other hand, due to their very nature, Helpers tend to become emotional sponges, soaking up the emotions of those around them, something they should be wary of. Since other's feelings cannot always be controlled or helped, people who fall into this personality type should be aware of the type of people they spend their time with to ensure that they are not soaking in too much negative emotion.

The Achiever

Type three, the Achiever, can also be called the Performer because when they are at their best, they can truly accomplish anything. Their strengths lie in being energetic and a high achiever which allows them to become very successful in life. To them, their own development, as well as that of others, is something that is valued the most. Most of the time, they are seen as the most popular person in the group because of their ability to stand in for others.

However, family or society defines success is what individuals with this personality type need to achieve in order to feel fulfilled, whether that is money or other status symbols. They learn to act in a way that will get them the praise and attention that they are always seeking.

The Achiever embodies the human need for attention and affirmation of value that most strive for, but not for the things that success can buy or the independence that will come with that. Instead, they strive for success because of their fear of being worthless and disappearing into some void which would only solidify that they hold no value.

The Individualist

The Individualist, or what is also known as the Romantic, is the fourth Enneagram personality type. This personality type is characterized by their belief that they are completely different from everyone else, making it impossible for anyone to understand or love them the way that they need. They have a strong conviction that they are in possession of singular gifts, but also that they are inherently flawed like no one else.

At their best, The Individualist is able to self-reflect and clearly see their motives and conflicts without trying to rationalize what they find, even if they do not like what they see. To them, there is no shame in admitting to things that may be shameful because they want to understand the experience in order to begin understanding who they are on a deeper level.

Unfortunately, their nature is such that they feel something missing from their lives or themselves, but they have trouble identifying what that something actually is. This leads the Individualist to admit that they do not necessarily have a clear picture of who they are; they lack a clear identity.

The Investigator

The fifth Enneagram personality type is the Investigator, or it can also be called the Observer because they are focused on amassing a large amount of intellectual knowledge. They always hunger for more information in an attempt to understand how the world works always testing things for themselves instead of taking information at face value.

Their need for knowledge often leads them to the life of a scholar or technical expert. An Investigator possesses a highly analytical mind with privacy and personal autonomy coming up at the forefront of what is most important to them.

An Investigator may be easily capable of detaching from the people around them, but that doesn't mean that they do not feel loneliness in that. Though they are highly intelligent and thirst for knowledge, relationships do not come easy. In order to continue on with their hunt for more information, they require adequate time alone, which means that time with family or friends will always come last.

The Loyalist

The Loyalist, the sixth personality type on the Enneagram, is the most loyal of all of the personality types. In other words, they will go down with the ship for their friends, hanging on to different relationships longer than most other personality types would. This loyalty extends beyond people into systems, thoughts, and ideas which they rarely challenge.

Loyalty may be a desirable trait; however, the Loyalist's main concern is not to become abandoned because they had different ideas than the people in their current relationships. Apart from loyalty, Loyalist also exhibits courage and giving attention to people as well as their problems.

On the other hand, they are also suspicious and pessimistic, which causes them to worry excessively. Overthinking causes them to be afraid to make any big decisions, but they also do not want anyone to make any decisions on their behalf.

The Enthusiast

Anyone who falls into this personality type can be described as enthusiastic, curious, and optimistic. Their wonderful sense of adventures means that they become enthralled with anything and everything that catches their attention. This overflow of enthusiasm for life ensures that they mingle in a couple of different projects at the same time, leaning towards those that will stimulate their brain to new things.

Defined as intelligent, they are very verbal with their thoughts even if they are not overly academic. Their brain's need for new stimulus makes them jump from one idea to the next with ease, giving them a great ability to brainstorm; however, they do not focus on the nitty-gritty of any topic. Instead, they thrive on being spontaneous, taking pleasure out of the general overview as opposed to an in-depth topic.

An Enthusiast quickly learns new things whether they are intellectual or manual, giving them the ability to become a master of many subjects. Unfortunately for them, their gift for learning gives them the problem of being lost—with so many things at their fingertips; an Enthusiast does not know what to do with themselves. Part of the problem is the ease with which they learn as it does not give them the time to appreciate a new skill they had to fight to learn.

The Challenger

Sometimes they are given the name of the Protector. The main component of this personality is how it got its name; they enjoy being challenged. They also enjoy challenging others and allowing them to reach their true potential. Individuals who are Challengers are charismatic, giving them the skills needed to get others to follow them.

To them, feeling alive comes from being able to use their strengths to bring changes to the world. In this, they also work on ensuring that though they are making changes to the world, they do not allow the world to hurt them in any way, as well as those they care about.

One of their priorities is fairness and justice since, in their world, a weakness can be exploited, and if they have been wronged in any way, they will fight back. This can be attributed to their fear of not wanting others to control them in any way. It doesn't matter to them what they become in life, whether it's the general of an army or the mother of five, they need to feel that they are in charge along with the added need to leave a mark upon the world which is unique to this personality type.

The Peacemaker

The ninth, and last, personality type on the Enneagram is the Peacemaker or Mediator. This personality is solely focused on finding the internal and external peace that can be applied to themselves as well as to others. They are often described as the glue that will hold a community together. The world is made up of mostly Peacemakers.

A Peacemaker has a strong desire to connect with the universe as a whole and work towards holding on to their peace of mind. Based on this, they are the most in touch with their physical bodies and the physical world, becoming out of touch with their own instincts.

Often being called the crown of the Enneagram, as it is placed at the very top, it seems to embody traits of all of the personality types below it. Most likely due to that fact, they do not have a strong sense of self, but instead, they melt into others. These characteristics of the Peacemaker means that they tend to try and numb themselves in order to find harmony, ignoring aspects of the world that they do not want to face.

How to Master the Spiritual Growth

A person is born on a specific time and day and is established into an astrological sign, house, cusp or other designation. To fully reflect on the traits and predilections of those under that category, you can investigate and strive to understand your relationship with the universe completely. This can be especially useful by raising your awareness of the past and the potential of the future, finessing your inner attunement with God. However, approaching astrology as a superstition can limit the use of this information and change this resource to a passive dependence on fate while you wait for the planets or stars to shift positions. Some people believe that religion and astrology cannot exist together as God is the only one who can have power or influence over your lifestyle, personality and future. Under this argument, if you are spiritual and can actually commune with God to receive answers on how you should behave and what your path is in life, there is no need for anything like astrology to guide you. Others believe that astrology can simply give you more information about your journey in this world and also with God, giving you further understanding and knowledge of yourself and those you interact with every day. Or it may separate from spirituality completely and use astrology as a way to dissect and study the universe, as it exists only through a cycle of cosmic principles and energy. Any of these approaches is a personal interpretation that everyone must make on their own. Aries: A Fire sign ruled by the planet Mars may need a physical spiritual practice, but with control. Yoga may be suited to this temperament, especially those types that are more energetic or vigorous in practice.

Taurus: the artistic Venus that brings out a gentle and creative approach to life. Most Taurus enjoy being in nature. This may lead them to feel a close connection to the Pagan religion. The celebrations throughout the year combining the spiritual with feasts and celebrations will speak directly to the heart of a Taurus. Having a close connection to the planet makes anyone under this Earth sign more enthusiastic.

Gemini: Gemini needs to be constantly mentally busy. This allows them to be more open to alternative approaches and spiritual discipline. The practice of mindful meditation, a Buddhist tradition, may help to quiet their mind and bring peace. With too much taxing the mind, the body can suffer as the nervous system can be pushed into insomnia and anxiety. The practice of turning off the brain and focusing on deeper connections is a great way to deal with stress.

Cancer: Cancer individuals can display a higher level of psychic awareness than other signs, especially if they have a history of family ancestors with similar abilities. Psychic pursuits, clairvoyance, aura readings and other similar fields may tune into the abilities and penchant of Cancer.

Leo: Leos have a lot of energy and need to be active daily. A spiritual practice that may appeal to them and that suits their temperament would be Tai Chi. Tai Chi is strongly linked to the Chinese philosophy and martial arts. It adds strength to the posture, deepens the breathing and has many health benefits. Leos will prefer Tai Chi classes to practicing alone as this will add a social aspect to it as well.

Virgo: Virgos need to be careful to engage in regular exercise and follow a diet. As their nervous system is an area of concern, they will benefit from regular practice. Alternative sources such as spiritual healing, aura reading or Reiki can be beneficial to this sign. Essentially, when participating in a spiritual activity, Virgos need activities that do not overly use their minds but can bring themselves out. It is assumed that among the twelve signs, Virgo is the natural healer. Virgo likes to give advice and service, so any spiritual or religious practice that includes doing good works would be close to their heart. However, any spiritual practice for a Virgo should allow them to recharge their mental batteries.

Libra: balance is their trademark. The study of auras might interest a Libra. Auras are the field that surrounds the physical body and are typically different colors which can display physical health, emotional well-being, and spirituality. The study and recognition of auras may allow a Libra to understand the actions of others better and teach them how to become more balanced when dealing with the other people in their lives. In turn, this may help them to build better relationships with people around them.

Scorpio: a spiritual journey will come as second nature to a Scorpio. During their lifetime, they may investigate a number of religions until they closely identify with one. With a drive to understand their life path and human psychology, they may experiment divination practices with Tarot to address the choices people face every day and properly decide on options that will make them move forward. The mysterious nature of the Tarot may appeal to a Scorpio to delve into the hidden aspects of the universe and life and to further understand the reason of why people live and thrive on Earth.

Sagittarius: this sign is known as the philosopher of the zodiac. They may be drawn to philosophy or a teaching role in whatever religion they choose. As they enjoy studying and exploring new ways of thinking and then sharing those words of wisdom, they may indeed venture into being a spiritual leader. Their journey into spirituality may involve Christianity, Hinduism, Buddhism or other alternative religion.

Capricorn: Although a materialistic sign, Capricorn does have the spiritual virtues that are required for a spiritual journey. Individuals under this sign need a spirituality that is going to last, combining both the need for being alone and spiritual advancement. Although less widely known, one option may be Shamanism. A Shaman alters the state of consciousness to communicate with the power of animals and the spirit world. Shamanism originates in central and northern Asia. This ancient and powerful spiritual practice takes time to learn, which will ensure a connection with Capricorn.

Aquarius: Aquarius is always looking up at the stars and to the future. Those under this sign may indeed be inclined to astrology. For those under this sign, astrology may be the key to self-understanding. Following astrology and finding the pattern through the planets and constellations may be a source of guidance to Aquarius. Once this pattern is revealed, Aquarius delves into a journey of joy and fulfillment and can take that lost knowledge to others.

Pisces: Pisces's personality constitutes their journey through their life and their spirituality. As the last sign of the zodiac, Pisces understands that we are just a small distance away from the next world. Pisces can contact the dead and possesses incredible psychic awareness. Pisces needs to learn self-discipline by energy cleaning and meditation. They are very sensitive with the surroundings and those that they come in with. To help steady their energy, it is best to give them some time to recuperate and be creative. This can lead them to a number of spiritual pursuits that connect them to that awareness such as Reiki healing, aura cleansing, meditation and more.

Aquarius, Pisces, Aries and Taurus

Aquarius — The Water Carrier

(January 20-February 18)

The first sign we will explore is Aquarius. Even though this sign is known as the water carrier, it actually falls under the air category. Air signs are thought to be social, communicative, rational and enjoy relationships with others. They are often quite friendly and intellectual. All positive traits come with some negative, and for Aquarius that is definitely the tendency to be somewhat superficial. The ruler of the Aquarius is the planet Uranus.

Pisces — The Fish

(February 19-March 20)

Unlike the water carrier symbol for the air element, Aquarius, the Pisces fish is a true water symbol. Their luckiest days of the week are Mondays and Thursdays. The ruler of Pisces is Neptune. They are generally compassionate, intuitive, wise and artistic. Pisces like, sleeping, spiritual themes, solitude, music and are usually quite romantic. They do not take criticism well, and loathe being witness to any kind of cruelty, or people who consider themselves a "know-it-all". Pisces also have a thing about the past coming back to haunt them, and often dwell on things that happened a long time ago. They are most compatible with Taurus, Cancer, Scorpio and Capricorn.

Pisceans are popular with just about any crowd because they are easygoing, and have a submissive nature about them that makes them less of a threat to those they associate with. They are most often selfless, and will help out others without expecting anything in return. As a water sign, they are quite empathetic and highly emotional. Pisceans are also compassionate, extremely faithful and caring individuals. A common trait that hurts their well-being is that they tend to concern themselves with the problems of others, rather than face and deal with their own.

This sign easily withdraws from reality, and prefers to spend a lot of time in fantasy worlds. There, they can do anything — from being rich and famous to living the life of a nomad; never settling down in one particular place. They often believe that their best work comes from the outside world, or the inspiration created by a muse. They find great pleasure in appreciating art, and yearn to travel to exotic places.

Downside to being a Pisces who can feel the emotions of others is that sometimes they worry themselves sick. They can also worry to the point that they are indecisive, and fear making a decision because they don't want others to disagree with them. This sign can easily forget to finish a task and might need a gentle reminder. They do not do well in managerial positions, but excel as support staff.

On the upside, Pisces are empathetic to the plight of others, and feel sorry for people whose lives are not going well. They usually believe what they are told, and try to reach out to those in need. They are caring people who feel deeply, even if it is not always apparent on the surface. They are creative and imaginative, and know no bounds when they are supported by their loved ones.

Aries — The Ram

(March 21 -April 20)

This fire sign is ruled by Mars. Aries are confident, optimistic, courageous, passionate and determined. They do well in leadership roles, and enjoy individual sports and physical challenges. They can also be impatient, aggressive, impulsive and short-tempered and will not find their calling in any role or job that they are not able to utilize their dynamic talents.

Although this sign begins in March, it is actually the first sign in the Zodiac. March 21 is the spring equinox, which is the beginning of the new zodiacal year, making Aries the sign of new beginnings. The ram is ambitious, impulsive, adventurous and energetic. They are usually very intelligent, and develop new ideas which they immediately want to put into action. They take on new challenges head on, but — because of their signature impatience — they can get agitated if results aren't immediate.

Aries make great, compassionate leaders in most fields. They are responsible, and have a genuine concern for their subordinates. Because they are a 'take charge' sign, they do not make good followers, and may actually be unwilling to submit to or obey directions.

Because this is the first sign in the Zodiac, Aries have a "lead-the-way-and-get-things-started" attitude. This also has to do with Mars being the ruling planet for this sign. Fire signs take action, sometimes before they've completely thought it through. Despite that, they have wonderful organizational skills, and don't like any sort of clutter in their environments.

Downside to this sign is when working a project, they focus solely on the goal alone, and can appear selfish to others. As mentioned, they are usually quite impatient, and if they are not promptly recognized for their hard work, they can become sarcastic and rude.

On the upside, this sign is highly energetic and willing to work long hours to complete a project. They generally take initiative, and in doing so, experience new discoveries and breakthroughs. Incredibly thorough, Aries have a knack for being precise. Their motto might just be, "live hard, play hard."

Taurus — The Bull

(April 21-May 20)

This sign falls under the Earth element, and is governed by Venus. Taurus are reliable, practical, devoted, stable and responsible. They are also known for their patience. With the bull as their animal, one might be led to believe that Taurus are aggressive when in fact, the opposite is true. Characteristically, Taurus are methodical and peaceful. Their actions are deliberate while relaxed, and they enjoy everything sensual. This includes food, sex, luxury and drink. Their love of luxury means that they will usually obtain it by working hard and purposefully. Taurus enjoy music, cooking, gardening and high-quality clothes. They are not fond of sudden change, insecurity or complications in work or life.

Taurus are incredibly stable, well-balanced and conservative. They are good citizens who obey the law and love peace. Because they love luxury, they are terrified to be in any serious debt, and will do everything they can to maintain their sense of security. This makes the Taurus hostile toward change. To them, the familiar is what keeps them in the lap of luxury, and they will always want to keep the status quo.

This sign is also very keen-witted, and often practical over intellectual. Once they've established an opinion, they are very unlikely to change it regardless of popular consensus. Their unwillingness to change their ideals makes them incredibly dependable and steadfast. They are just, and can keep their cool in the face of any difficulty.

On the downside, they are stubborn and unwilling to change the ideals they've adopted. This can make them quite difficult to get along with, especially when it comes to cooperating on a project in school or at work. In social situations, they are leaders that prefer to be held in high esteem. If they are not, they might refuse to work and could try to find ways to sabotage relationships or projects. Although they value the law and follow it, if they see an authoritative figure they deem unworthy to lead, the Taurus might seek to sabotage them as well.

On the upside, Taurus finish what they start. It is rare to see them leave something undone. They think deliberately, and when they make a decision, it tends to be the right one. If there is a reward of luxury or anything sensual, they can be adaptable. They are very family oriented, and love to spend time with their loved ones.

The best matches for Taurus are; Cancer, Capricorn Pisces and Virgo.

Gemini, Cancer, Leo, Virgo, Libra, Scorpio, Sagittarius and Capricorn

Gemini — The Twins

(May 21-June 20)

Gemini and the Lovers

Number 6 is related to Gemini in Astrology, more popularly known as the "twins". You probably are a born communicator, and you do know how to speak your mind well.

Gemini is partly brainy, but could also be scatterbrained, and this is why you have to learn how to make use of introspection, and numerology to help yourself feel better. However, once you learn to know yourself better, you can be one of the funniest, most exciting people around.

You might also be quite flirty, and could be someone who tries to use his charm to get his way, or make his way out of certain things. One thing that you do have to remember, though, is that you have to learn how to slow down and calm your mind so that you won't easily be distracted of what's happening in your life.

In Tarot, this number is associated with The Lovers, which also says a lot about how you choose a partner in life.

What this means, though, is that whoever you decide to be intimate with, you should be fully committed. This is also why you have to "study your options" first so you'd be sure that you're with the right person, especially if a long-term relationship is in your mind.

Be mindful of the choices you'll make, especially if you know they're going to bring forth some discontent. Always learn to stick with your choice, and don't be too fickle-minded—or you just may hurt yourself and some people too.

Cancer — The Crab

(June 21-July 22)

The Number 7 is associated with the Cancer sign in Astrology. This means that you have the tendency to be quite sensitive, mostly because you are ruled by the emotional moon. While you have this tough exterior, you may also be the kind of person who keeps his feelings hidden just to avoid getting hurt, which may also mean that you're not really living life to the fullest, and thus, you're often said to be "crabby".

This could be changed, though, when you meet someone—or even a group of friends—who really gets you for who you are, and whom you can be sincere with. You may also be naturally protective, but at the same time, you may have crazy mood swings that you have to try to prevent from happening, if you can.

Try to manage and process these feelings first before reacting or you may just overreact.

Meanwhile, when it comes to the Tarot, this sign is connected to the Chariot, or someone who parades himself as a "hero" along the streets. What you have to understand is that even though you may be "on top" now, it doesn't necessarily mean that it's what's going to happen forever. Therefore, you have to learn how to be open to changes, and understand that life isn't always a constant thing. Learn how to be receptive to the new people in your life, as well. This way, you can "travel light", and just allow yourself to glide through life better.

Leo — The Lion

(July 23-August 22)

Next is number 8, which in Astrology is associated with the Leo sign. Leo stands for the Lion, which means that you could be quite fiery, and are someone who cannot easily be ignored. You are quite charming, and also has the love for drama, and naturally has a warm spirit, and is quite hospitable.

You are an actionable person—you don't like just to sit around and do nothing, and you often make sure that you do what you can to live life well. However, you could be quite attention-seeking and arrogant.

In Tarot, this number is related to Strength, which determines your nature in its most primal form.

You could be quite persuasive, especially when it comes to what you want in life. You also have to learn to distinguish your ego from your true self, and you should separate enlightened wisdom from self-interest. Have some integrity so you could influence others in the right manner, so that this way, you will succeed with whatever you have in mind, as long as it is good, of course!

Virgo — The Maiden

(August 23-September 22)

The Number 9 is related to Virgo in Astrology. Also known as the Virgin, this means that you can be quite analytical, detail-oriented, and ultimately hard-working, and you kind of get to see what's wrong with certain people or with their environments right away. However, the problem is that when some people start critiquing you, you do not take to it too lightly, and you may easily turn your back on them when this happens.

Therefore, you have to try to lessen the perfectionism and just try to be a realist—after all, no one is perfect, and it's always best to just do your best, instead of seeking to be "perfect" and destroying everything you have put your heart and soul into before.

In Tarot, this number is associated with the Hermit. This means that you're able to recognize those people who could teach you a thing or two about life—otherwise known as your life teachers or mentors. You are the kind of person who gains wisdom from your experiences in life, and from the people you meet, and who make an impact in your life.

One thing you have to remember, though, is that you have to try to think things through, and that you have to be careful of the way you think, as well. This way, you get to understand the more essential things in life, and learn to see the bigger picture. You also need alone time, so do not be scared to tell people that you need to be alone for a while, think, and then just get your ducks in a row.

Libra — The Scales

(September 23-October 22)

Duality (Masculine Feminine) - Assertive

Element - Air

Quality - Cardinal

Ruling Planet — Venus: Just like the name of the famous Goddess, this planet is linked to pleasure and beauty. In addition to aesthetics, this also includes sociability, harmony, attraction, and eroticism. Venus changes signs every four to five weeks.

Dominant Keyword - I BALANCE

Polarity - Yang (+) Libras are very level-headed and do not get angry easily, so when they do, it is usually for a good reason.

Part of the body - Kidneys, Skin, Lower Back, Buttocks

Lucky Day - FRIDAY

Lucky Numbers - 7, 20, 55, 77 and 86

Magical Birthstone - Chrysolite

Special Colors - Pink and blue

Flowers - Rose

The danger for the people with that sign — Financial success is not a priority to Libras, and they will have many ups and downs when it comes to their careers because of this. Libras place more value on peace and justice in their lives.

Scorpio — The Scorpion

(October 23-November 21)

Duality (Masculine Feminine) - Passive

Element - Water

Quality - Fixed

Ruling Planet - Mars (ancient) and Pluto (modern): This tiny planet represents how people cope with power, both their own and other people's. Pluto is associated with transformation and rebirth, which also includes the cycle of death and regeneration. Pluto's orbit causes it to change signs every twelve to fifteen years. However, this can vary.

Dominant Keyword - I DESIRE

Polarity - Yin (-) When Scorpios are young, they are often religious and virtuous, but when they reach their twenties, they will undergo a dramatic shift. Many of the greatest saints were born under this sign. Even though it is common for a Scorpio's mind to change and for them to seek new experiences and paths, sometimes they dedicate themselves to their faith and feel as though they found their purpose early on.

Part of the body ruled by Taurus - Reproductive System, Sexual Organs

Lucky Day - TUESDAY

Lucky Numbers - 27, 29, 45, 53 and 89.

Magical Birthstone - Beryl

Special Colors - Black

Flowers - Chrysanthemum

Metal -Water

The danger for the people with that sign - they are infamous for procrastinating and will look for any excuse to put something off until a later date. This is not the best habit to have in the business world, so they must learn to adhere to a schedule if they want to be successful. However, once they overcome this obstacle, they are usually very successful in the career they choose.

Sagittarius — The Centaur

(November 22-December 21)

Duality (Masculine Feminine) - Assertive

Element (Fire, water [..]) - Fire

Quality - Mutable

Ruling Planet – Jupiter: Jupiter embodies hope, faith, luck, spirituality, justice, and purpose. Jupiter also represents spiritual growth and wisdom, and it changes signs every twelve to thirteen months.

Dominant Keyword - I SEE

Polarity - Yang (+) Sagittarius love to travel and learn as much as they can, they find it enlightening and fun. They are also known to be carefree and independent, but for the right partner, will make love a priority in their busy lives.

Part of the body - Hips, Thighs, Liver

Lucky Day - THURSDAY

Lucky Numbers - 6, 16, 23, 60, and 81

Magical Birthstone - Citrine

Special Colors - Purple

Flowers - Narcissus

The danger for the people with that sign - This sign is prone to restlessness because they have trouble sitting down and relaxing. They get bored easily and prefer instant gratification where they can get it. When a Sagittarius faces a task or goal that takes longer than anticipated to accomplish they move onto something else altogether and forget about the initial task. Even when they are 'relaxing,' they are making plans, and it is for this reason that they are so good in a crisis.

Capricorn — The Mountain Sea-Goat

(December 22-January 19)

Duality (Masculine Feminine) - Passive

Element (Fire, water [..]) - Earth

Quality - Cardinal

Ruling Planet — Saturn: This planet represents our limitations and boundaries. It explains the way a person experiences "reality," and the places they meet resistance in their lives. Saturn is also associated with laws, rules, morals, and our conscience, and whether we choose to abide by laws or regulations. Saturn is also connected to our concentration and our powers of endurance, including reserve and caution. Saturn only crosses through a sign every two or three years.

Dominant Keyword - I USE

Polarity - Yin (-) Those born under this sign are eyes on the prize types that let nothing stand in the way of them fulfilling their purpose. They take the concept of destiny and work very seriously and put great faith in their own abilities. They are mentally sound and strong, but often not understood by others. They excel at government work or business ventures but do not do very well being at the bottom of the corporate ladder.

Part of the body - Joints, Skeletal System

Lucky Day - SATURDAY

Lucky Numbers - 3, 21, 66, 83, 84.

Magical Birthstone - Ruby

Special Colors - Brown and grey

Flowers -Carnation

The danger for the people with that sign - Fear is at the root of a Capricorn's troubles; this is a life-long battle they fight with themselves. Learning to cope and overcome their fears is something that they must learn to do. However, this does not always come easily, and part of it is usually finding the patience and inner calm to allow themselves to begin the long process of chipping away at these fears and frustrations. Everyone has different fears, but for a Capricorn, it generally deals with failure, living without purpose, and feelings of loneliness.

Celestial Sphere

If on a clear night we turn our eyes to the sky, we will see an incredible number of stars, bright and not very, and it seems that there are so many of them that it is not possible to make out something in the sky. But if we take a closer look at the set of diamond points in the sky, we will notice that some of them form separate groups1. How to navigate the starry sky map

In antiquity, people distinguished groups of stars: the imagination of a certain sage gave these groups diverse forms. There are purely geometric shapes, but more often people used the shapes of animals, people, or objects. Then the name "constellation" appeared. In the northern hemisphere there are special constellations that shine only for Europe; There are special constellations in the southern hemisphere, on the other side of the equator.

Star route 1 Description of stars and constellations. A star is a part of the constellation that could be distinguished.

It is worth noting that in addition to stars that invariably appear in the sky, there are moving celestial bodies, the path of which passes through the constellations. This is the Sun and the Moon in the first place, we will talk about other planets later. Let us linger briefly on the external manifestations that the Sun and Moon project onto the Earth.

We will notice that most of their movements are due to the movement of the Earth, but for now we will leave it so as not to get confused.

Thus, people noticed that on its way through the sky the Sun crosses the constellations, each time the same; they also noted that the moon moves on the same principle as all other wandering stars or planets.

Zodiac

This path along which the heavenly wanderers move is called the path of heavenly animals, or the divine starry path, or the zodiac. The zodiac consists of twelve constellations. Knowledge of the zodiac is essential for both the astronomer and the astrologer.

Sky division

All celestial bodies are divided into two large categories: motionless stars, from which constellations are formed, and wandering stars, which move through the twelve signs of the zodiac.

Motionless stars

In fact, motionless stars can only be called relatively: they really do not move independently - this distinguishes them from wandering stars. But the sky moves around the Heavenly Pole; therefore, ancient people believed that the sky is like a huge ocean, in which the constellations rise and go.

Celestial sphere

The set of astronomical observations, both ancient and modern, is based on the sunrise and sunset of the constellations.

Celestial sphere according to the ancient system of Ptolemy

To navigate the sea, people divided the celestial sphere into parts by analogy with the division of the Earth. Between the two poles and through the center passes the celestial equator; The zodiac, which acts as an ecliptic in the sky, divides the equator into two parts so that the six signs of the zodiac are above the equator, closer to the Arctic pole, and the remaining six signs are below the equator, closer to the Antarctic pole. The northernmost sign of the zodiac is Cancer, the southernmost is Capricorn.

In the sky, in addition to the equator and latitudinal parallels, there is another belt that passes through the sign of Capricorn and is called the Tropic of Capricorn. The two aforementioned zodiac signs, Cancer and Capricorn, are the northern and southern extreme points of the zodiac, respectively, and form the line of the winter and summer solstices; the other two signs, eastern Aries and western Libra, make up the line of the spring and autumn equinox.

Four corners symbolize the beginning of the four seasons. Now you need to remember the order and names of the zodiac signs. Please note that the astrological year begins in March.

    Aries (A) March 20 ………… April 20

    Taurus (B) April 20 ………… May 20

    Gemini (C) May 21 ………… June 20

Cancer (D) June 21 .... July 22

Leo (E) July 23 .... August 22

Virgo (F) August 23 .... September 22

Libra (G) September 23 .... October 22

Scorpio (H) October 23 .... November 21

Sagittarius (I) November 22 .... December 21

Capricorn (J) December 22 .... January 20

Aquarius (K) January 21st .... February 18th

Pisces (L) February 19 .... March 19.

These dates indicate the entry of the Sun into other signs in 1916.

In small portions you will learn the sequence of zodiac signs, which is extremely necessary for astrology.

For a better understanding of the arrangement of the zodiac signs, we recommend using a special mnemonic reader:

OV - TE - BLI - RA

LEO - DE - WEIGHT - SPORTS STRE - KO - WATER - PY

Each of the twelve signs of the zodiac is a group of closely spaced stars, enclosed in a geometric shape. In antiquity, signs were assigned symbolic images of animals, characters, or objects that they were like. In addition, each sign was assigned a symbolic image, and we advise the reader to remember them.

We will continue, but let's learn what we have already learned about the signs of the zodiac. This knowledge gives us the opportunity to consider them further in the future.

How each Planet's Astrology Directly Affects every Zodiac Sign

In astrology, zodiac signs get a lot of attention— after all, to read the regular horoscope, all you need is a sun sign. But the field of astrology is big, light, and majestic, and if you want to see what the stars are trying to do in astrology, you need to get an understanding of what planets mean. It's not a surprising news that planets are something in the field of astrology— after all, it is precisely what astrology is. To perceive the passage of planets and other celestial bodies through the heavens (and zodiac). Yet knowing the planets will help you make so much more sense of things like your signals of sun and moon, and in the next moment, someone rants about Mercury going backward again, or their location of Venus ruining their life of love.

You are undoubtedly still familiar with the planets of the old solar system (shouting out to teachers of primary school science around the world). Nevertheless, you have a seat back at your office, as planets in astrology can vary a bit from what you discovered from Bill Nye, the Science Guy. Next, both the sun and the moon are called planets in astrology. Although in the astronomical sense they may not be stars, they are vitally critical celestial bodies for all of we earth dwellers and therefore called planets as far as astrology is concerned. Pluto is also a satellite in astrology. While astronomers may have demoted it a few years ago to a mere dwarf planet, it's still a full-fledged planet in astrology— and it's just as strong. Finally, scratch the Earth from the list of planets in astrology— I mean, it's essential, but we also live on it, so from our Earthly point of view, it doesn't travel through the sky like the other celestial objects. All in all, ten main planets are made up of that.

Through astrology, each planet represents a different set of qualities and characteristics and rules another part of our lives— each taking their unique vibes with them. "Each planet symbolizes another part of life, another form of energy," Astro Library explained. "In psychological terms, we might call them' needs' or' drives.'" The planets ranging from the earth to Mars are known as' inner planets.' We pass relatively quickly from sign to sign, thereby providing greater control over every day, shorter-term problems. "Outer planets," ranging from Jupiter to Pluto, travel even slowly through the zodiac table, thus affecting higher parts of your life and yourself. And when someone names a planet "beneficial," it refers to their association with delivering perfect vibes (Jupiter and Venus are regarded as beneficial). On the other hand, "malefic" planets like Saturn and Mars are believed to have stronger, more destructive energy (although we love them and still need them!).

Okay, it depends on where they are located to learn how the planets impact us. Planets pass through numerous signals, and their energy works out differently depending on their location. If you want to learn where your birth planets are, your birth chart will need to be checked out (if you have your precise birth date, you can find it online, or ask a qualified astrologer to help). The birth map consists of twelve astrological houses and twelve signs of the zodiac that correspond with those houses. But there are stars in all these signs and buildings. "That house provides the planets living there with a home — giving the planet a place to practice its unique energy," Insightful Astrology explained. But planets do not affect anything themselves— it's more about where they are located and how they communicate with other parts of your map.

Sun

Naturally rules: Leo

The sun is our universe's nucleus. It's what the world around us paints, the light around which we revolve, and that brings us beauty. That's part of why, and who we are, our sun signs are so crucial to our astrology! "The Sun is our conscience, our life-force, what we are motivated to do," Stardust says to Bustle. The sun is the driving force behind our hearts, and people who can accept their sun placement tend to feel happy and satisfied.

Moon

Naturally rules: Cancer

The sweet, emotion-driven moon is seriously our Astro mom (I know I'm a mad Lil' witch and all, but I practically welcome the moon with a "Hello, mum!" when I see her in the night sky.) "The Moon reflects our inner feelings, the pieces within us which we cannot communicate," says Stardust. "It also reflects our maternal side, our parents, our memories, and what foods we love." Nurturing, receptive, and governing over matters of survival, the moon rules over the dark, more fragile aspects of ourselves, as well as the factors we need to feel safe and comfortable.

Mercury

Naturally rules: Gemini & Virgo

You probably know this world more than anything else for its notorious retrograde cycles, but in truth, this fast-witted master of contact is cool when it doesn't turn anything upside down in your life. "Mercury impacts how we interact, communicate and travel information," McGarry says to Bustle. Mercury is known as the gods' messenger, so it makes sense that it is its jam to connect, share information, and fly.

Venus

Naturally rules: Taurus & Libra

Beautiful Venus, a flowery, sensual, and heart-flutteringly wonderful world of all things. Named after the divine goddess herself, Venus enjoys life and is absorbed in the world's aestheticism and aesthetics. Venus is also synonymous with money— especially the money we spend on things that offer us pleasure and joy more frivolously. "Venus portrays love affairs, passion, elegance, fine wines, and rich food," Stardust says. "Venus always embodies self-esteem and wealth." She's kind of like the planet's Valentine's day — think of a romantic evening full of chocolates, champagne, red rose petals, and a warm bubble bath.

Mars

Naturally rules: Aries

Wild fiery Mars is strong, motivated, and full of raw, unbridled, animalistic fire, named after the god of war. "Mars is the way we fight and show ourselves," McGarry states to Bustle. The so-called Red Planet, with its red-hot strength and zeal, definitely lives up to its name. And you might have noticed "Mars guys, Venus women," right? Okay, we all have a delicate balance of both, so while erotic passion is the domain of Venus, Mars rules over our sexual drive and attraction that is more animalistic. In our gut and feel, Venus is the butterflies, while Mars is the primitive physical impulse.

Jupiter

Naturally rules: Sagittarius

The bigger the head, the closer to heaven, the larger the world, the closer to sweet, sweet peace, as the saying goes. Jupiter is considered particularly auspicious, carrying with it its vast presence of prosperity, positivity, potential, and good vibes. "The greater benefit of Jupiter is an opportunity, prosperity, travel, spirituality, schooling, teaching, and expansion," says Stardust to Bustle. This big boy is a positive and good luck spreader, so always welcome the peachy vibes of Jupiter.

Saturn

Naturally rules: Capricorn

If the moon is our celestial mother, then Saturn is our cosmic lord altogether. Speak of this world as the harsh father who is a little too rigid, oppressive, and strict. "Saturn is the biggest malefic, representing limits, boundaries, limitations, and parental partnership," Stardust states. About the notorious return of Saturn, which happens to everyone around their late twenties (cue utter existential breakdown), you may be familiar with Saturn. Saturn's all about tough love— but mind, it's just harsh on us because we want to learn and grow.

Uranus

Naturally rules: Aquarius

Look forward to the unpredictable with Uranus as this planet is about shaking up the standards. It is radical, forward-thinking, hyper-creative, but susceptible to abrupt changes and transitions as well. "Uranus is known as the' Great Awakener' as it shakes the universe on a universal level through revolutions and creativity," says Stardust. For nostalgia, Uranus doesn't care about tradition— it cares about being pioneering, bright, and unique. The world is sometimes compared to a beam of light because it surprises us with unexpected discoveries and inspirations.

Neptune

Naturally rules: Pisces

Dreamy, Neptune, otherworldly. The origins of this world are as profound as their color is blue, as they reflect psychic imagination and spiritual attainment, as well as visions and artistic expression. As Stardust states, "Neptune reflects visions, imagination, and myth." Because of its dreams, inter-dimensional existence, it also appears to separate itself a little bit from reality. But if you can avoid falling into this planet's escapist habits, it will offer a positive resilience and spiritual power.

Pluto

Naturally rules: Scorpio

Scientists back in 2006 may have stripped Pluto of his planethood — indeed a cruel move, particularly to the planet named after the king of the underworld. Yet Pluto is as planet like as it can be in astrology. As McGarry tells Bustle, "Pluto includes the transition force."

Transition covers a lot of ground — think of the energy of light and darkness, death and rebirth, day to night, culminating in the beginning. Like Anne Welles said in the Valley of the Dolls, "You have to scale Mount Everest to reach the Valley of the Dolls." And if the Valley of the Dolls is your inner reality, then hey, brace for the daunting so dangerous yet exciting war that Pluto insists on, because it is undoubtedly for the ultimate good.

Oracle Cards and Psycards

Oracle Cards

Oracle cards are very similar to Tarot cards, with one exception—there are no rules to follow with oracle cards. Much like with Tarot, these cards are used to gain clarity, inspiration, insight, and answers. These cards are just more modern than Tarot. Like with Tarot decks, there are many different styles of oracle decks to choose from, and you should pick one that resonates with you and that you can connect with.

Since oracle cards do not have any rules, it is a very freeform way of getting guidance, checking if you are on the correct path, receiving clarity and inspiration, and getting questions answered. Oracle cards are all about how you feel when you look at the words and imagery on the cards, and both are equally important. There is no set number of cards you need to draw, no set-in-stone meaning—all of this is so that the interpretation is completely up to the reader. Many find it helpful to write in a journal while pulling cards in order to keep a flowing stream of consciousness. Many find this allows them to get what they want out of reading more easily.

A historian, Caitlín Matthews, is very familiar with oracle cards, particularly the 36-card Lenormand deck that was named after Mademoiselle Marie Anne Lenormand, a famous card reader from the 18th and 19th century. The cards were not published with her name until after her death, and the two oldest Lenormand-style decks in Matthews' collection are the French Daveluy from the 1860s and the Viennese Zauberkarten from 1864. The Zauberkarten decks were some of the first divination decks that used chromolithography to produce the imagery on the cards.

Oracle decks rely on a visual language that is more direct than those that traditional Tarot cards use. Most fortune-telling decks, like thee Lenormand deck, focus less on archetypes and tend to use straightforward imagery that keeps the conversation more direct, as opposed to Tarot cards that speak in a universal language that is broader.

A woman by the name of Mary Greer found that there was a predecessor to the Lenormand cards called "les Amusements des Allemands" or the German Entertainment. These were created by a British firm, and the Lenormand decks heavily resembled their style.

Popular oracle cards are:

- The Angel Blessings Oracle Card Deck
- The Deck of Shadows Oracle Card Deck
- The Earth Magic Oracle Card Deck
- The Magical Unicorn Oracle Card Deck
- The Wisdom of Avalon Oracle Card Deck
- The Mystic Art Medicine Oracle Card Deck
- The Sacred Path Oracle Card Deck
- The Black Power Tarot Oracle Card Deck
- The Animal Kin Oracle Card Deck
- The Spirit de la Lune Oracle Card Deck
- The Cosmic Mother Oracle Card Deck
- The Illest Oracle Card Deck
- The Rebel Oracle Card Deck
- The Ancient Animal Wisdom Oracle Card Deck
- The Angel Answers Oracle Card Deck
- The Cards of Alchemy Oracle Card Deck
- The Celtic Oracle Card Deck
- The Moonology Oracle Card Deck
- The Wild Offering Oracle Card Deck
- The Goddess Power Oracle Card Deck
- The Earth Magic Oracle Card Deck
- The Precious Gems Oracle Card Deck

- The Every Day Oracle Card Deck
- The Whispers of Lord Ganesha Oracle Card Deck
- The Goddess Guidance Oracle Card Deck
- The Wisdom of the Oracle Divination Card Deck
- The Sacred Rebels Oracle Card Deck

Psycards

Psycards were influenced by Carl Jung's work in psychotherapy and can be used to get answers and guidance, help with one's growth and self-improvement, and deal with a question that has been on your mind for a while. They were created by Nick Hobson and Maggie Keen in the 1980s.

These cards work similarly to Tarot, but this deck only has 40 cards instead of 78. The cards do resemble the Major Arcana, but they are separated into 6 groups:

- Directions
- Happenings
- Characters
- Fundamentals
- Archetypes
- Symbols

The symbols are used to link the unconscious and the conscious mind, allowing you to get answers to direct questions and receive general guidance. If you do prefer to receive general information, there is a simple spread you can do:

- Shuffle your cards
- Draw 7 cards and put 2 in a row on top, 3 below that, and 2 on the bottom
- the top row represents what you should aspire to.
- the middle row shows the past, present, and future.
- the bottom row shows the forces that are unconsciously driving you forward.

Performing Tarot Readings

There are a few differences between reading for yourself and reading for someone else, so these will be covered before we get into the process of a Tarot reading.

Reading for Yourself

Some Tarot readers will tell you that you cannot read for yourself, but it holds little merit if you believe that the Tarot is simply there to help you tap into the information that you already subconsciously know.

When you are reading for yourself, it can be a useful tool in personal self-discovery and development. When you are first starting out, reading your own Tarot is a great way to learn and familiarize yourself with the cards. A great idea is reading your own Tarot every day and keeping notes over those readings in your Tarot journal.

Since you are reading for yourself, though, it can be difficult to remain objective and emotionally removed. Doing this, however, is incredibly important, as your emotions and attachments to the situation can hinder your ability to read correctly the cards you draw. Meditating beforehand, whether to clear your mind completely or simply focus on the question you have, can do wonders for the remaining objective. You can also choose to use an inanimate object to represent yourself and set it across from you (where your client would sit if you were doing a reading for them), and tell yourself that the reading you are doing is for this '"you," sitting opposite you.

Many people, especially those who are just starting out, find it beneficial to do their reading out loud, just as they would do with a client because it enables them to see things that they may have missed by just looking over them in their head.

Reading for Others

When reading for others, the rules are similar but different. Instead of shuffling the cards yourself, it can be more beneficial for the querent to shuffle them. This is because it gives them the opportunity to infuse their own energy into the cards while thinking about the question they want to be answered.

When you decide to read for others, you will have to keep in mind that their skepticism can play a big role in how well the reading goes. If a person is a non-believer, that doubt can skew the cards or make them useless (unreadable) gibberish. It can also end up being a waste of time if the querent believes the reading does not relate to them or that the things the cards have said will not happen. The best thing to do in situations like this is to end the reading, as it is not benefitting anyone, not you or the client.

It is also important that you take into consideration what the client or querent can and cannot handle. This was covered in ethics, but it is an important consideration to keep in mind. Your job is never to lie to the querent if there is bad news; simply determine the best way to tell them in a way that will not crush them. Putting a positive spin on something or offering them options to fix the situation will always soften such blows.

For example, if someone's reading produces the Death Tarot card, assure the client that it often means death in the way of an ending, but all endings happen to make room for new beginnings. There is typically always a way to put a positive twist on a reading or particular card, and it is the reader's job to ensure that the querent leaves feeling empowered and not beaten down.

If you happen to get stuck in a reading, it will typically resolve itself as you look at the other cards, so if you need to skip a Tarot card and come back to it, that is completely acceptable. Often, doing this actually makes the once confusing card make perfect sense, and all you needed was a bit more context clues to figure it out. If that is not the case, and you are still stuck, you can use the tips that are listed:

- First impressions
- Describing the Tarot cards
- Searching for patterns
- Drawing a clarifying card
- Giving yourself or the querent time

Reading for Family or Friends

After having practiced on yourself for a while, you may want to spread your wings a bit and branch out to a few people you are close to so that you can practice in a judgment-free environment. Being able to practice on family and friends who are close to you is definitely a benefit, as it gives you more practice and exposure to the cards, but there can be a few hindrances that come along with that as well.

Since these people are typically close to you, you tend to know their stories, and you know what is going on in their lives, making it difficult to remain detached in the way that you should in order to perform the most accurate reading. Much like when you are reading for yourself, reading for those whom you are close to can be difficult because of the emotional ties you have to the situation, even if you are not directly linked to the question they want to be answered.

Meditating and clearing your mind can help you remove yourself from the situation while reminding yourself to be objective can also do more than you might imagine.

Reading for Strangers

If you decide to read for others in a business sense, you will often do readings for people whom you do not know. Now, this can be both more or less ideal or easy, depending on who you ask or what kind of person you are.

The emotions and connections that you have with family and friends can make it pretty difficult to give a good, accurate reading, but there is the level of comfort that comes with it that some could find as a plus.

Reading for strangers certainly eliminates the emotional connection, as you will not know anything about their life. This typically makes it significantly easier to interpret the story that the cards are attempting to get across to you, as they are not being blocked by bias or non-objectivity. You are free to use your intuition to determine what the cards are trying to say and the wisdom they are trying to impart upon the one who seek.

Note for Readings for Others

When you start doing readings for others, whether your family, friends, or clients, you will move through the five numbers of their Core Profile, and there are some important things to keep in mind.

Always start with the Life Path Number, and explain to your participant why it is the most important number in their profile. Then, move on to the Soul Number, to reveal what their heart wants: This is the private, more intimate side of them that only those very close to them get to see. Touch on compatibility by explaining Soul Stress Numbers (here).

From there, look at the Personality, Destiny, and Birthday Numbers. These all have a profound effect on career and how one makes a living. Discuss the special gifts, talents, and abilities this numerical energy grants them.

Follow with the Attitude Number, explaining this is where first impressions and judgments are born. Finish with the Maturity Number, which becomes more relevant depending on the person's age.

While you are doing the reading, pay special attention to the placement and influence of each number. If there are repeating numbers in the chart, discuss those intensities. Repetition can significantly change the meaning of the information you relay.

Explain Karmic Lessons and Debt as they are revealed, and always offer gentle guidance about how to learn lessons and pay the cosmic bank. Empower them with the tools to resolve karma during their lifetime.

Close with the cycles and timing of their Personal Years, Months, and Days in order to give them awareness of the opportunities, possibilities, and challenges that may come their way.

BE SENSITIVE AND RESPECTFUL

Doing readings for others comes with immense responsibility. Think about who usually asks for a reading—generally, people seek help in times of despair or when at an important crossroads. They are looking to the spiritual world for guidance. Consider it an honor and a privilege to provide guidance during such times.

Clients, friends, and family might make important decisions based on the information and insights you provide. Because of this, you must be careful with your words and never project your personal feelings, judgments, or opinions into the reading. Remember that you are just a conduit for the intelligence the numbers provide.

Keep it positive. Avoid creating self-fulfilling prophecies for your clients or friends. For example, if you find markers for divorce in a chart, don't doom the person to give up on a relationship as soon as it gets hard (there's always room for interpretation: this is also the marker for someone who is widowed or has lost a parent at a young age). Instead, explain they may experience some harsh lessons around love. You never know exactly how the numbers will play out in another person's life. As the always inspiring Maya Angelou said, "Words are things, I'm convinced. You must be careful." You cannot undo the power of a word once spoken. Bring kindness, empathy, and compassion; these traits will be some of your greatest assets as a reader.

If you choose to showcase your new knowledge as a party trick, be respectful of the science. Always make sure you are accurate and have a clear mind (math and alcohol don't usually mix well). Many intuitive believe that if the gift is abused or used in the wrong way, their abilities will be decreased or even blocked.

Some clients will take everything to heart; others will struggle against it. Free will is always involved, and people will heal only when they are ready.

I cannot emphasize this enough: Ground your energy. You do not want to take on someone else's problems or toxic energy, so implement boundaries. There are many effective techniques and crystals that offer protection. Continue with your own research and find a method that works for you.

To quote Numerologist Hans Decoz, "Numerology is a difficult, but intensely rewarding profession." Motivate, inspire, elevate, provide insight, and always tell the truth, and your readings will be fabulous!

DEVELOPING YOUR INTUITION

Your intuition will continue to evolve and expand along with your awareness and confidence. Understanding and developing intuition is deeply personal and happens differently for everyone.

Early in my Numerology career, I was taught the concept of "blah"—basically, receiving a very strong message that you blurt or "blah" out (which stands for "bring love and healing").

This phenomenon has created some of my most meaningful and heartfelt connections with clients. Several stories come to mind, but I'll share just one:

That nagging message came to me as the words "blue plaid shirt, blue plaid shirt." I tried to dismiss it, but it was relentless, as messages from the Universe tend to be. Eventually, I asked the client the significance of this image. They had no immediate answer, so I continued on with the reading. By the end of our time together, her face lit up and she ran out to her truck to get something to show me, a program from her father-in-law's memorial. It had a photo of him in a blue plaid shirt.

I still get chills when I think about how emotional this was for her.

Finding the balance between kindness, honesty, and censorship will be crucial. Check your ego, keep everything confidential, and deliver your intuitive readings with compassion and love.

CRACKING THE CODE

Whether you choose to reveal your new ability is up to you. People can get strangely secretive about their birth date (or even provide inaccurate information) when they feel you could reveal something that they'd rather keep private. With experience, you will likely know when this is the case. Never push someone to share their numbers with you. Always be open to learning, respect boundaries, and keep an open mind.

Eventually they'll understand what you know after reading this: that life can be easier, decisions and timing less confusing, and relationships more harmonious and greater opportunities can be seized through Numerology.

Embrace the magic of the Universe. I've often said that if everyone had just a little Numerology in their lives, the world would be a more magical, understanding, and compassionate place.

Congratulations on your newfound wisdom.

Tarot 101- Getting Started

Now that you're ready to get a Tarot deck and begin the learning process, the first thing you must do is find your own Tarot deck and make it your own. You can then start to develop a personal connection with those cards and build a foundation that will provide you with guidance and insight for years to come.

- Choosing a Tarot Deck

Because there are so many Tarot decks now available, it can be difficult when first deciding which deck to use. Don't worry about choosing the wrong deck, as anything that calls to you is going to the right fit. You aren't limited to just having one deck either, you can and probably will end up with multiple decks that you use for various reasons. Some will keep one deck private, and only use it when they are reading cards for themselves. Others will use one deck for everything. Most teachers of Tarot recommend that you find a deck that you resonate with and use it to practice and learn with. Once you are comfortable enough to perform readings for others, you will know if you require a new deck for that purpose or if the one you already have will work.

No matter which deck you end up choosing, having a sense of connection with it is crucial. Take your time and browse all the options available to you. If you find a deck and decide that you don't really have any relationship with the images, find a new deck. You're not held to any commitment with the Tarot. Once you locate a deck that you like, you'll want to clear the energies that might exist around it and cleanse the deck. If that sounds a little too metaphysical for you, think about as introducing yourself to the deck and starting fresh.

- Sorting

To begin, you will want to sort out your cards and pay attention to any energies that you might pick up from them. On a clean table or area, sort your cards out in front of you in order. Start with the Major Arcana cards and then sort the Suits of the Minor Arcana. Take a brief look at each card while doing this. This is a way of ensuring that you have all the cards in your deck as well as taking note of the illustrations for the first time. When dealing with the Minor Arcana cards, sort the Suits by type and then by number. You start with sorting in order from Ace through Ten followed by the Page, the Knight, the Queen, and finally the King card.

For the purposes of learning, you may want to sort your cards into the Major Arcana and the Minor Arcana and put one or the other away in the place you dedicate for storage. When we focus on either one of these specifically, we allow space for further insight and development. For example, it's quite common to start with the Minor Arcana and to develop a good sense of what each Suit, Number or Court card is telling us. It makes us focus solely on a limited number of cards so that we can use the repetition to build on our original thoughts and impressions.

- Cleansing Energies

Once you have looked at each individual card and have it sorted you can use a smudging wand such as sage or sweetgrass to clear any stored energy in the cards. This is particularly useful if you have cards that have been used before, but it's also a great starting point for new decks. At this point, you may want to meditate on the cards and visualize energy coming from you and moving towards and into the cards. If you're familiar with guided meditation or visualization techniques, you may want to use them to create a protective circle of while light that encompasses you and the cards. This can be a powerful cleansing and connection exercise.

There are energy cleansing techniques that are much more involved such as salt burials, moon bathing, or water clearing. If you feel your cards have any negative energies associated or clinging to them, take the time to perform a cleansing ritual with them. For beginners though, a simple sorting and pause in contemplation should suffice. It's recommended that you do some sort of energy clearing, however small, before performing any readings to concentrate on the questions at hand and the client.

- Making the cards your Own

When you are satisfied with the energy, pick them all up and shuffle them to impart your own energy into the cards. Continue shuffling and reshuffling any way you like to achieve this. Maybe you want to shuffle a certain lucky amount of times or randomly select cards to put on top or at the bottom of the deck. Whatever works for you will get your deck ready for its first use. When your deck is not being used, you should consider where you will store them. Many people find the box that they came in completely okay while others have a dedicated, specialized space just for them. Silk is associated with magical properties due to how it's created and is widely accepted as the fabric of choice when wrapping cards before placing in a box. While it's fine to do what feels right for you, keep in mind that Tarot is an ancient art that deserves our respect and reverence.

Develop a Personal Connection

Now you are ready to work with your cards and develop a personal connection to them. This connection should be with every single card in the Tarot deck. You may choose to begin with the Minor Arcana and develop a sense of what each Suit represents. You may decide to start with the Major Arcana and develop an understanding with the illustrations found there. However, you go about learning the cards for the first time, you'll want to associate meaning to each one. You will begin to develop a relationship with your cards, which is why working with a deck you like and resonate with is so crucial. You're basically bonding with the deck and noting how you feel when using it.

You don't have to memorize the meaning of each card, only develop a basic sense of what the card represents at first. You will inherently acquire a sense of what they mean as you continue to work with them. Keep in mind that you will at one point want to express what they represent to other people so work on creating associations that are easily recognized, repeated, and deciphered. This should be fun for you, so if you feel that it's becoming too much information just take a step back and return when you are ready. You don't have to learn the whole deck right away; you can pull one card and sit with it until you feel ready to move on. Some people select only one card and meditate on it and learn everything they can from it for an entire month. This can take a very long time but if you are serious about using Tarot for deeper insight, it's a practice that is highly recommended. Remember that you can do this as you practice daily.

For now, any symbolism and representation that you find in each card are completely fine. Lay out all the cards and with a birds-eye-view take note of any patterns that emerge. Keep a journal of themes that the cards share and feelings that they give you. Refer to your journal throughout your learning to build upon your relationship with them. The interpretations of each card are only activated when you are interacting with them. When you have a need for the indications, you will be ready to find them and use them. Use this time you are spending bonding with your Tarot cards to develop your own opinions about them. The deck you chose essentially becomes an extension of your voice. Be honest with anyone that might approach you for a reading early on. Let me know that you can do it for fun but that they shouldn't take anything that comes across seriously as you are just learning. Remember, these meanings are hypothetical and not necessarily prophetic. You and the people you may do readings for are safe from harm.

Shuffling

Learn to Shuffle your Tarot deck. Unless it's very small, shuffling a deck can be difficult. This is because the cards are larger and thicker. There are many ways to shuffle a deck successfully- just keep in mind that if you are spreading them out and circulating them repeatedly that you do so on a clean surface where they will not be damaged. You can attempt to shuffle them like a regular playing card deck, or try shuffling half of them at a time, etc. You can cut them repeatedly, or have your client cut them. The goal is to have the cards be completely randomized while you're contemplating the questions being asked. This is the difference between getting a meaningful reading and not just random cards to interpret.

When you are performing a reading for someone else, consider letting them shuffle the deck so that they can get in tune with their energies. If that's not something you're comfortable with, that's okay! Maybe you can compromise by letting them cut the deck as many times as they want to without ever fully handling your cards. Discover where your boundaries are regarding your cards and demand they be respected.

You can always pick up a spread and reshuffle the deck and re-spread them. If you are not connecting with the person asking the questions, or you are not in a headspace to interpret the cards you'll find that reading the Tarot cards is hard to do. Clear the energy around you and on your cards and begin again. You do not have to pull meaning out of the cards forcefully. This should take exertion on your part as the cards will provide the insight you are looking for just by sight. You can develop intuitive reading quickly through practice!

Decks for Experienced Readers, Collectors, and Tarot Lovers

Tarot de Marseilles

This traditional French medieval style deck is a must-have for any collector who loves history. It is one of the oldest deck designs still in popular circulation; its earliest version may have been produced as early as the year 1500; there is a copy of this deck still in existence that was made in 1650. In the Tarot de Marseilles, illustrations of the Major Arcana cards are somehow cartoonish simplistic and hauntingly beautiful at the same time. The only reason this deck is not ideal for beginners is the design of the numbered suit cards; while they are beautiful and intricate, they often feature geometric designs rather than illustrations and can be difficult for novices to interpret.

Mother peace Tarot

This is one of the most popular and distinctive modern decks around. It was designed in the 1970s to update the classic Tarot imagery to something better suited to new-wave feminist ideals, particularly inspired by the Goddess movement. The cards are round rather than rectangular; their shape symbolizes the moon and feminine energy. This is a wonderful deck for those who crave a diverse, intersectional, feminist update to Tarot imagery and symbolism. The deck even has its own unique spread of eleven cards laid out in a circular shape.

The Hermetic Tarot

Another great deck for history lovers and those with a special interest in the esoteric side of Tarot. This deck features a great deal of symbolism from the Secret or Hermetic Order of the Golden Dawn, an occultist group that was popular in Europe at the turn of the twentieth century and still survives to this day (though it boasts lesser numbers currently). While the current Golden Dawn movement may have some unfortunate connections to fascist and racist ideologies, the Hermetic order was primarily concerned with the preservation of ancient alchemical, cabalistic, and arcane knowledge; current leaders of the Hermetic Order claim no connection or alignment whatsoever with the modern Golden Dawn movement. This deck is a wonderful tool to further your study of individual card meanings, as the images feature clues to elemental, astrological, Kabbalistic, numerical, and geomantic connections for many cards. The entire deck is drawn in only black and white, with highly detailed illustrations; you'll want to stare at these spreads for hours.

Aquarian Tarot

This deck is breathtakingly beautiful, featuring art deco and art nouveau inspired illustrations and a modern color scheme. The symbolism is a bit more complex than a standard deck, and this isn't ideal for a novice cartomancer, but for a reader who has some experience with a traditional deck, it will be easy to transition into this style.

Shadowscapes Tarot

This is a gorgeous deck, with finely detailed, ethereal illustrations. In fact, the beautiful imagery is the only reason this deck might not work for beginners--it can be a distraction, and furthermore, some of it is quite abstract. This is a great deck for anyone who loves fantasy, Norse mythology, and faeries.

The Wild Unknown Tarot

This beautiful deck is gaining a large modern following. It may not be best for novices, as many of the illustrations are minimalist, featuring nature and animals rather than human characters, but the artist's interpretations of card meanings are profound and inspiring.

Starchild Tarot

A perfect deck for the modern-minded wiccan, this deck uses a gorgeous pastel, new-age color scheme, and photo-collage art to create some truly breathtaking imagery. This deck draws heavily on cosmic spirituality, sacred geometry, metaphysical healing philosophies and ancient mystery schools for symbolism.

Fountain Tarot

Another wonderful modern deck, the Fountain Tarot features original oil paintings by Jonathan Saiz that beautifully capture the concepts of Tarot, updating them for the internet age while retaining a sense of mystery and appreciation for its historical legacy. It's a must-have for modern metaphysical practitioners, energy healers, and contemporary art lovers, too.

Visconti-Sforza Deck

This deck is about as old as the Tarot de Marseilles design, and another wonderful deck for history lovers, with illustrations drawn in more of a medieval style, barely hinting at the dawning of the Renaissance. The original Visconti deck is missing four cards--the Tower, the Devil, the Three of Swords and the Knight of Coins--so for modern prints, these four cards have been recreated in a similar style to the rest of the deck. Many of the original cards survive to this day, in museums and private collections; they were often created using precious materials, such as gold leaf for the card's borders, and show us not only that Tarot was valued by the wealthy and powerful, but also provide us a glimpse into the daily life and value structure of the Italian nobility of the 15th century through its detailed imagery.

Caring for your cards

However, you acquire your deck (or decks), you'll want to store them in a silk cloth or bag, in a cool, dry place. Ideally, you'll want to store them out of direct sunlight, but also avoid storing them in perpetual darkness (basements, dark corners, etc.). If you believe in metaphysical power, then be sure to protect your cards from negative energies, either by storing with a crystal that can combat negativity, keeping the deck within a protection grid or by regularly cleansing the cards.

In order to bond the cards of the deck to your personal spirit, see to it that nobody touches the cards except yourself--even those people whose questions prompt your readings. For this reason, it might be wise to purchase another deck for practice after receiving your first as a gift; that way, you can work with another novice to familiarize yourself with card readings.

Some cartomancers believe that Tarot decks, even when wrapped in silk and out of use, possess the metaphysical energy needed to weaken or even open portals between realms easily; for this reason, some warn that Tarot cards should not be used or even touched during pregnancy, or while a woman is menstruating, and that decks should also be avoided on All Hallow's Eve, on nights with no moon, and any evening after ten o'clock at night, if the reader wishes to avoid communion with any negative energies or malicious spirits.

How to cleanse your cards

Especially after practice or heavy use, you'll want to make sure that you cleanse your decks to remove any negative energy and prevent muddled clarity in the messages you receive from the cards. If you aren't using your Tarot decks frequently, you'll still want to put them through a routine cleanse about once a month; get into the habit of cleansing every new moon, or every full moon if you prefer to use moonlight for cleansing.

To cleanse with moonlight, spread your cards out beneath the light of a full moon and give them time to soak up those moonbeams--at least an hour per card--before wrapping them in silk again. Another popular cleansing method is smudging, which is a ritual cleansing with smoke. This can be done by burning smudge sticks made of bundled sage leaves, rosemary, or any other dried herb with a scent that you particularly enjoy. Run the cards over the smoke, being sure to separate them so that the smoke can reach every single card, on all surfaces.

Alternatively, some cartomancers prefer to slip their decks into plastic bags or airtight containers before burying the sealed deck in salt (ideally, sea salt or rock salt, but table salt will also work in a pinch), making sure the deck is entirely submerged, and remains buried for several days before being used again. This method takes longer, as the salt will slowly draw negative and stagnant energies from the deck as it would draw moisture from a piece of preserved meat. Be sure to keep the cards protected in an airtight container, as salt and moisture may damage the cards over time.

Awakening your intuition

One of the first steps towards enhancing your intuitive powers is to learn how to recognize them. Many of us make the mistake of thinking that intuition happens in the head or mind, as part of a thought process; that is intellect, not intuition. Intuition happens within the body and subconscious. It often displays itself as strong emotions or physical sensations. An inexplicable sense of optimism, a melancholy mood, or a sudden sharp pain in the gut--these experiences can all be interpreted as intuitive messages. Meditation and mindfulness practices are excellent tools to heighten your awareness of intuitive experiences and can help to transform you into an astute and insightful card reader, as well as helping you to become the best possible version of yourself in other walks of life.

Lots of people are imbued with many more intuitive gifts than they give themselves credit for, especially since modern life and technologies often encourage us to disconnect from and deny our gut instincts, suppressing physical manifestations of emotion. This being the case, it is usually a good idea for a novice cartomancer to spend some time reflecting upon the imagery in their first deck before they begin a formal study of Tarot. Go through each card in the deck; examine the illustrations; maybe even grip each card with both hands, creating an energetic channel, close your eyes, and breathe. How does the card make you feel? What messages can you divine from it without external guidance? Different decks have different energetic vibes, so while this will speak to the most commonly accepted interpretations of popular decks, you may find that your cards depict the mysteries of life in a different light, or capture them from a different angle. The colors and shapes used in card illustrations will impact you on a visceral level, and these initial impressions will resonate even more strongly with a reader who gets to know their deck without any preconceived notions or expectations.

Many card practitioners find that they benefit from ritual practices to deepen their connection to their favorite deck, leading to more accurate and insightful readings. You might incorporate your deck into a daily, weekly, or monthly meditation practice, holding the entire deck or just a single selected card as you meditate on its imagery and divine meaning. You might also adopt the practice of sleeping with your deck underneath your pillow (wrapped in silk for protection, of course!) to connect your dreaming, subconscious mind to the cards.

Dream journaling can be extraordinarily helpful in enhancing your awareness of your intuitive mind; it can also aid the novice cartomancer to get into the practice of interpreting imagery and symbolism in abstract sequence. Spending time in nature, relaxing, and regular sleep cycles are immensely important for divination; without a healthy, well-rested mind, even the most experienced card-reader is liable to misunderstand the messages of the divine and their own subconscious.

Sense isolation can be a useful practice for recognizing and honing your sixth sense. Sensory deprivation chambers can provide this experience for a cost, but you needn't shell out any cash to experiment with this practice. Try using makeshift blindfolds, earplugs or nose plugs, or keeping your hands bundled in oven mitts to learn how acute your senses can grow when one or more of the others are diminished. This can help you to recognize where your sensational feelings are coming from, and root out those that have no rational or obvious explanation.

For those who struggle to quiet the mind during meditation, repetitive actions or tasks may be able to provide a similar transcendent experience. This could be running, practicing the performance of one particular song on the guitar or piano and striving for perfection, chopping vegetables to prep meals for the week, doodling, juggling, dancing, or creating origami sculptures. These repetitive motions can lead you into a sort of self-induced hypnosis.

The Effect of Numerology on Your Life

You have taken the journey of finding out how Numerology and specific numbers impact you as a person. Numerology doesn't just affect you, though, it also affects the things in your life as well. It has an influence on what paths or choices you may make in regard to life, career, and love.

Influence on Life Path

Your life path is the essence of your life. Every challenge, opportunity, and lesson during the span of your life is related to the Numerology behind the life path number. If you want to know where your life is essentially going to go and what you are going to face, your reading with your life path number can tell you.

Influence on Your Personality

Your personality is the DNA of who you are. The personality number that Numerology uncovers about us it the core of who we are as a person. Every action we take, every situation we face, and how we handle it, all aspects of our personality. Numerology readings regarding your personality show you exactly who you are as a person, and no matter how we try to fight it, our personality is something we were born with and it is impossible to deny it.

Influence on Career

Choosing a career path is influenced directly and indirectly by our Numerology. We are people who are composed of so many different traits that once our reading is complete, it can show us where we were naturally born to rule. Think of it in terms of those tests that we were all made to take in high school. The ones that supposedly shows you what profession you are supposedly made for. Your Numerology numbers do something like this but consider your total person, not just who you are on the surface.

Influence on Our Interests

Because we are all composed of different traits, we are naturally made to enjoy certain things while detesting others. This works the same vice versa. When we know who we are and who we are meant to be based on our numerological makeup, it is easier to accept and explain the things that other people may find abnormal in our lives.

Influence on Attitude

The first thing that people tend to notice about another person is their attitude. There is a good chance that the way you come across to other people can be explained in greater detail based on your numerology reading. We are all composed of different numbers and paths, which can have a severe influence on our attitudes. Someone may interpret an attitude that is strong-willed as being defiant when in reality, you are simply focused on your goals.

Influence on Relationships and Compatibility

Besides the incompatibility that you learned with the Zodiac, there are also incompatibilities that occur with the Numerology numbers as well. There are a lot of things that are required to make a relationship with someone else work, and sometimes what happens is that we are simply just not compatible. Personalities can clash just like the courses we want to take with our lives can clash. It would not be any one person's fault if the incompatibility were naturally destined to happen due to the incompatibility of Numerology readings.

Influence on Location

It is proven that every city and state have their own numerological vibration, which means that if you have ever felt out of place somewhere, chances are you were not compatible with the numbers. Before changing your scenery, it might be worth talking to an expert numerologist to find out about the vibrations of the place you are thinking of moving. Much like relationships, it is not your fault for feeling averse to a place. You are just not numerically wired to belong there.

Influence on a Home

Just like the vibrations, a location can possess, the same can apply to your new address. Your home or apartment can have its own numerical vibrations, and if you are not compatible with it, you may never feel at home. It might be worth your time to get a Numerology reading for your potential home just to make sure that you are compatibly going to be comfortable.

Influence on Pets

Your pet is a person too, so in the same way that you have numerical vibes, so does your pet. The name you choose can have a huge influence on their personality, thanks to the vibrations from the name and the astrological values predestined for them. You can find out your pet's reading by using the same Numerology calculations done on your own name.

Influence on Business Ventures

The name of your business can be converted into a numerological reading as well. Just like you and your pet, the path that your business name falls under will be an indicator of the success or wealth it may attain. If you and your business's life path numbers are compatible, it can prove to be extremely prosperous for you.

How to Read Astrological Chart

Simply put, an astrological chart is the projection of the sky on the Earth's plane. Of course, that the Earth is not a plane, but this is not the question here because we approximate the image of the sky onto ourselves as if we were the center of the world. And if we "catch" the image of the sky at the same moment we were born, then we have the "natal chart". The same is applicable for the charts of the animals, buildings, companies, business deals, events like weddings, receptions and anything you can think of. These are all natal charts and they all describe the potential for good and bad events, which can happen further on, depending on some other factors.

The main one of those "other factors" are planetary transits. They are the most important fact in western astrology; while the Vedic school favors divisional charts, which is an arrangement of the planets and sensitive points in the chart calculated through some geometrical and mathematical rules. To avoid confusion, you should know that Vedic or sidereal astrology deals with sidereal positions of the planets in the sky, while western astrology deals with tropical positions or the projection of planets on the Earth's plane. In simple words, for example, the first day of spring is March 21st. We know this because day and night are equal and this is called the spring equinox. The Sun enters into the sign of Aries and the new cycle begins. You know that this is the equinox; you know that spring is here, but if you go to the observatory and look at the Sun through a telescope, you will see that Sun is still in the constellation of Pisces. This "effect" is happening due to the precession of the equinoxes; however, for now this concept is beyond the basics of astrology.

The most important thing you have to know is that both astrological schools are right, they have their precise prediction systems, which differ, but they both work. The quality of the prediction depends on the quality of chosen astrologer, not the school which is selected for the reading.

Let's get back to planetary transits. This is the term which describes the image of the current or upcoming planetary arrangement in the sky. If you, for instance, overlap the transit chart over your natal chart, you will be able to see the areas where you are challenged, blessed, where can you grow, in what to invest, from what or who to beware and so on. Sometimes the warning signs are extremely obvious if you know how to read those two sets of planetary arrangements together.

The same applies to your partner's charts, whether they can show the development and the outcome of love, business or any other relationship. All you need to do is to overlap those two charts and to read mutual aspects that the planets make.

GENERAL ASTROLOGY RULES

First, you have to know the meaning of each planet and the meaning of each astrological sign. Then you have to know the basic aspects planets make together.

The chart in the western astrology style is presented as a circle divided into 12 parts, each one representing astrological houses. The most important points are the Ascendant – Descendant (Asc-Dsc) line, which is a horizontal line in the chart and the Medium Coeli – Imum Coeli (MC-IC) line, which is showing the highest and the lowest points of your chart. Those are four of the most important points you have to pay attention to. Ascendant is your rising sign, describing just you. Descendant is how you deal with your love, business or any other partner and how you project yourself into the world. IC is your origin, while MC is your highest accomplishment.

A circle with the cross in it, it is so simple, and the whole life in it.

The image of your natal chart will look like this circle, but with the snapshot of the planetary arrangements at the moment you were born. This snapshot holds the potentials which will develop to a greater or a lesser degree, depending on upcoming planetary transits during your life. Whether those potentials and life's events are good or bad, you will know by reading the aspects the planets make.

PLANETARY ASPECTS

Whenever celestial body moves through the heavens, it creates a motion, frequency, and sound. Any relation between celestial bodies creates a mutual aspect and all together they make the music of the spheres. However, the aspects considered as the most important in astrology are conjunction, sextile, square, and trine and opposition.

Conjunction happens when the two planets are placed close to each other so their influences are mixed. If there are three or more planets involved, then this is called stellium. Are the planets forming conjunction or stellium? This depends on their orbs of influences. Bigger bodies have greater orbs and for the Sun, Moon, Jupiter, and Saturn, this can extend to 15 degrees because they are big planets with great strength. Also, depending on the planets involved, conjunction can be considered as good or bad.

Sextile is formed between planets when they form the 60-degree angle between them looking from the center point of an astrological circle or a chart. Generally speaking, this is a good aspect and suggests that planets are active and can result in a positive outcome.

Square happens when two planets form a 90-degree angle in the chart and squares are often perceived as bad aspects because they can bring very challenging situations in our lives. But, at the same time, they force us to change and to grow in attempts to overcome or resolve our problems.

Trine is seen as the exceptionally auspicious aspect and it happens when two planets form a 120-degree angle between them. Although beneficial, trines can sometimes produce a lazy attitude, so there is really nothing just black and white going on in the sky.

An opposition is another "bad" aspect because two celestial bodies are forming 180-degrees angle and they are directly opposing each other. This is challenging too, causing open war between opposite sides, frictional, but at the same time, it provokes the search for a better option or solution.

ZODIAC SIGNS AND HOUSES

Now that we have learned the general meaning of planets and aspects in the chart, we should take the closer look at the astrological signs and houses. As you already know, the horoscope is divided into four sectors (remember the cross in the circle?) and twelve "houses" or main areas of life. In Vedic astrology, those houses are equal. Each one extends to 30 degrees. However, in the western school, this is not the case, because the geometry of the point on Earth where you were born, for instance, is calculated through various systems. This is something which is beyond the basics, but you should know that today, Placidus house system is mostly used and it shows the best results, except in the case that person was born in the areas of polar circles.

The main rule of astrology is that each Zodiac sign has the meaning of the same house. Translated, this rule can be easily explained looking at the signs. Aries is the first sign in the Zodiac belt, so the first house of any horoscope has the general meaning of the sign of Aries; the second house has the meaning of Taurus and so on until we reach to the Pisces or twelfth house.

For instance, you can be born in the sign of Gemini and this means that you were born on the 21st of May until 20th of June. However, if you were born, let's say, during the afternoon hours, your rising sign or your Ascendant could be placed in the sign of Scorpio. This is just an example; we will have to know the exact time to see where the Ascendant is placed.

Now, you have your natal Sun in Gemini, but your rising sign is Scorpio. This means that your first house is placed in the sign of Scorpio, but at the same time, this means that you will have all the traits of Aries (first house) through the characteristics of Scorpio. In this case, also, the Sun is placed in Gemini, but in the eighth house of the horoscope, which again carries the symbolism of the sign of Scorpio. Add to this mix the position of your natal Moon and you will have the basic understanding of your character and appearance.

It can sound a bit complicated for an absolute beginner, but in time and with the little practice, you will start using those "double" systems, not even thinking about them while applying the rules.

True Purpose of the Zodiac Sign in Life

The signs of the Zodiac can give us incredible experiences in our everyday lives, just as the numerous gifts and uncommon characteristics we have. You can find a lot of important data about yourself by finding out about your Zodiac sign. In this article, we'll disclose to you how you can utilize the data gave by your sign so as to improve your life.

The term zodiac indicates a yearly cycle of twelve stations along the way of the sun. Astrologists utilize galactic perceptions of the developments in the night sky for divinatory purposes. Each star sign has a different significance, and your astrological chart is comprised of the sun signs and their traits, and the position of the planets in the place of your exceptional chart.

Your Sun Sign could be either sign since the date changes marginally from year to year. If you were conceived inside 2 days of the sign change dates, you might need to counsel an astrologer to discover your actual Sun Sign.

Every zodiac sign mirrors a different side of your own encounters and character, despite the fact that some of them are more underlined than others. In view of the date of birth, a spot of birth and time of birth, astrologer can give you an extremely exact representation of your character, just as reveal to you numerous things about your past and future, gifts and difficulties. Individuals from all societies accept that astrology is one of the absolute best devices that there is for understanding a person's latent capacity, qualities, and shortcomings.

Every one of the Zodiac signs is additionally designated into components. How these components identify with each other is particularly significant when utilizing astrology to decide an adoration coordinate. Astrologists accept that every individual is good or incongruent with others dependent on their introduction to the world dates. To characterize this similarity, your component bunch is contrasted with the other component bunches in the zodiac chart.

Those brought into the world under the Zodiac signs Aries, Leo, or Sagittarius have a place with the component of fire which speaks to excitement and solid will. The earth component incorporates Taurus, Virgo, and Capricorn, which speaks to useful and material concerns.

Aquarius, Gemini, Libra, and emanates from the air part and address ratiocination. The water component incorporates Cancer, Scorpio and Pieces and speaks to sentiments, feelings, and sympathy.

Your Zodiac sign can give data that can assist you with having a more joyful existence by drawing out into the open your qualities and shortcomings. If your sign makes you inclined to envy, you can deal with being additionally trusting.

If you're destined to be a pioneer, you can concentrate on excelling expertly. Numerous individuals start their day by counseling their horoscope to perceive what the day will bring. That demonstrates that the intensity of the Zodiac is still particularly alive.

The Most Effective Method to Understand Your Horoscope

As you likely know, a horoscope is a guide of the sky at the time you were conceived. Your horoscope gives the astrologer what indications your planets are in. It uncovers every one of your propensities, dispositions, dissatisfactions, gifts, and life reasons. Also, significantly more!

Be that as it may, you don't have to make sense of this to discover what your Mars implies. Simply ask an astrologer.

Suppose I took a glance at your horoscope and discovered that your Mars is in the sign of Cancer. Here's a simple method to get this:

Mars = enthusiasm and want to make a move

Cancer = a sign that identifies with nourishment, heating, bread, land, home, family, stomach, mothering and supporting

Presently, put a portion of these implications together with Mars, and you will think of a few things you truly have the energy for. At that point, you basically solicit "Which one of these things, that identify with my energy, do I feel the most grounded about?"

You may state that you have solid energy for cabinetmaking, which identifies with building homes. Or on the other hand you could have solid energy for land or running a bread shop. Regardless, your Mars in Cancer shows that your enthusiasm is firmly related to the everyday issues that identify with that sign.

Here's another model:

Your Mercury is in Aquarius. Mercury = thinking and correspondences.

Aquarius = identifies with cutting edge innovation, PCs, airship, space travel, astrology, designing, melodic structure, and kinships.

If you have your Mercury in Aquarius, you will consistently move toward data from a specialized or propelled level of awareness. The Aquarian signs bestow a sharp capacity to look past the undeniable and search out radical types of articulation. A portion of our most noteworthy pioneers, designers, and authors had Mercury in Aquarius.

If your Mercury is in Aquarius, the entirety of this will sound good to you.

Don't you discover it very astounding that the sky can uncover such a lot of data about you?

We should take one more model.

Your Venus is in Leo. Venus = gratefulness, fascination, what you like. Leo = sign of expressions of the human experience, imagination in all structures, love, sentiment, sports, theater, painting music, the heart, and kids.

If your Venus is in Leo, you are genuinely sentimental. You love the round of adoration, exploring every available opportunity, and conveying everything that needs to be conveyed imaginatively. You have a caring heart and you need to give that feeling to other people. At the point when you join the planets with the signs, think about the planet as want and the sign as a disposition. At that point, your horoscope will start to sound good to you.

Clearly, your horoscope is definitely more mind-boggling than this, yet I have indicated you in an exceptionally basic manner how the planets and signs uncover what your identity is.

Astrological Terminologies and Their Meaning

If you are new to astrology, then it is fundamental to get familiar with a portion of the essential terms that are utilized in astrology. This would assist you with understanding and pursue your introduction to the world chart. Each term decides some importance. Here are the terms and what it signifies given in a point by point way. The air horoscope image is the signs of Gemini, Libra, and Aquarius. Ascendant is the term signifying the rising sign. This is the horoscope image on the cusp of the principal place of the birth chart. Relative is the cusp of the seventh house in the birth chart. The horoscope image of Taurus, Virgo, and Capricorn are called Earth signs. Components, which are outstanding to all and it is said to be Fire, Earth, Air, and Water.

Aries, Capricorn, Cancer, and Libra, symbols are referred to as 'cardinal signs'. The horoscope image of Cancer, Scorpio, and Pisces are water signs. Aries, Sagittarius, and Leo symbols are referred to as 'fire signs.' Gemini, Virgo, Sagittarius, and Pisces symbols are referred to as 'variable signs.' The horoscope image of Taurus, Leo, Scorpio, and Aquarius are said to be a fixed horoscope image. Cancer, Capricorn, Pisces, Scorpio, Taurus, and Virgo are referred to as 'feminine signs.' The other Zodiac signs are referred to as a 'masculine horoscope image.'

Every one of these signs has its own highlights. In the horoscope, a few divisions are seen; it includes twelve in number. The paradise is separated into 12. These are called the houses and each house is managed by specific planets which are called planetary rulers. Each house likewise signifies some specific everyday issues. What is referred to as the luminaries are the Sun and the Moon? A cusp of a sign is said to be the degree when one sign closures and different starts.

The cusp of the principal, fourth, seventh, and tenth houses are said to be the quadrants. Zodiac is a hover of 360 degrees. The 360 degrees variant of Birth chart is partitioned into 12 equivalent divisions of 30 degrees each. You can see this plainly in any birth chart. It is difficult for a non-specialist to comprehend these terms. An astrological individual has total information on what these terms allude to. Nowadays, CDs are accessible in the market which gives data about these astrological sciences. Indeed, even online channels assume a significant job as it gives a wide range of astrological data at the fingertips. However, the opportune individual must be counseled who might be the best source to control you altogether.

Expression Number

One

An individual with the number one is often very skilled in the world of business. They have a natural tact for entrepreneurship and often have grand ideas for new businesses they want to start. This individual will probably have many successful (and a few failed) businesses in their lifetime. They greatly enjoy being their own boss and many are known to find ways to live from home. Individuals with this number can also be very hypercritical of themselves or others. This can help create a quality business or organization, but if the individual does not keep this trait in check, they can push away those around them. People may find them overly judgmental or too harsh of a critic. Paying attention to this trait and learning to reign in their opinion will help maintain good, comfortable relationships with coworkers.

Two

Individuals with this number put a lot of weight on social prowess. They tend to be very skilled in the world of manners and elegance. These individuals usually have very high social skills and are very talented at marketing themselves and others. These people usually make brilliant marketing professionals and excel in the world of advertising. The hardest pill for this person to swallow is the fact that not everyone is going to like or get along with them. These individuals want to be friends with everyone and often cannot handle it when someone either clearly or secretly dislikes them. It would be beneficial for this person to remember that sometimes there is nothing you can do to make someone like you. These individuals may need to try and let it go if someone simply isn't getting along with them.

Three

Individuals with this number usually have increased skill in communication with others. Because of this, they tend to make brilliant writers, actors, and artists. They can often communicate feelings and emotions in a beautiful and elegant way that can be understood across a wide array of platforms and media. These individuals are often found in careers that involve some sort of self-expression because that is what they love to do. The flaw often found in these individuals is that they may have difficulty concentrating their thoughts into clear and concise information. They tend to go off on tangents and ramble for long periods. An individual with this number usually has to do a lot of editing to their writing and can often end up with mass amounts of cut material that has almost nothing to do with the end product. These individuals would benefit from thinking more clearly about what they are going to include in their projects and taking a moment to consider more deeply if it connects properly to what they are trying to convey.

Four

Individuals with this number often have skills in management and organization. They are often fair and impartial leaders who thrive in structure. These individuals are known for being reliable and consistent in their lives. These individuals tend to reject the unconventional and like to live in stable, structured environments. These people tend to find themselves in nine to five jobs where they have some sort of managerial status. Risk takers, these individuals are not. They are not likely to take jobs for companies that are up and coming or that appear to be rapidly growing or shrinking; they prefer to find employment within a well-established company. These individuals are faithful and loyal to those close to them. The biggest negative to this person is their tendency to focus too hard on the things that are outside their grasp. They tend to get caught up on the barriers that block them from things that they want and would benefit from focusing more on the things that are within their capabilities.

Five

These individuals are quite the separation from their neighbor, number four. These people live for adventure and love excitement. They practically ooze curiosity and are known to throw themselves into every new mini obsession they develop. They despise structured and organized careers and would rip their hair out in a typical nine to five job. These individuals crave freedom and constant stimulation. These individuals' greatest talents are their ability to pick up random unusual skills seemingly out of the blue. By working hard, these individuals can learn how to do anything from fixing a car to juggling. Because of their charismatic and energetic demeanor (and their love of travel), these individuals often have a large group of friends from very different cultural and geographic backgrounds. Fives, unfortunately, tend to have a higher chance of becoming addicted to things like alcohol, drugs, and even sex. Their need to experience new and interesting things can often have consequences that they either don't notice or outright ignore at that moment.

Six

Individuals with this number are often very committed to speaking up for the underdog. They usually are the pushers of political movements and have a talent of getting others to agree with them purely through their conviction. These individuals are often known to be extremely passionate about the things that they are involved in. They are usually representatives or heads of nonprofits. From time to time, these individuals tend to put others before themselves too much. That is to say – they tend to push their needs and skills to the side to accommodate those which they believe to need help more. It would be beneficial to these individuals to remember that they are important as well and should focus more time and energy towards themselves.

Seven

These individuals are often very analytical and usually quite skilled at finding answers to complex questions. They usually make brilliant scientists or engineers. These people are usually very skilled at mathematics and science because they have a rare ability to see every detail and remember every last part of a process. These individuals are known for having a strong urge to seek the truth in everyday life. They are constantly asking questions about why things happen and are usually inclined to find the answer no matter what. These individuals are very determined to understand the world around them and often find that if they have not found the answers they seek, by a certain age, they may sink into a difficult depression. These individuals would benefit from remembering that some things in life are not meant to be understood.

Eight

Individuals with this number have only one goal in life: to win. These individuals are extremely competitive in almost everything that they do. They want to be number one in everything and are willing to fight hard for it. These are the type of people to turn everything into a competition, but they are also the type to work the absolute hardest for something they want. The greatest skill of this individual is their ability to focus on an end goal and push themselves past their current fatigue to reach that goal. These individuals care very little about their own comfort in a given situation. These individuals sometimes tend to work a little too hard and should remind themselves that it is often more important to take a break than to finish something.

Nine

Individuals with this number are often described as being philanthropic and a humanitarian. They are often very passionate about the activities they are involved in. These individuals are very powerful in their belief in themselves. These people often believe so strongly that they can accomplish anything that they usually do. It is these individuals' pure willpower that sets them apart from the crowd. They are often their own champions and have no trouble cheering themselves on their whole life. With this strong high can sometimes mean a strong low as well. This means that while these individuals believe very strongly that they can do anything, if they are not able to do something important to them, they may fall into a deep depressive state.

Life Paths

Life path number

This number is the negotiator and the arbitrator of any cause and effect that occurs in your life. This number determines you experiences in the world and can also be described as the way by which you project yourself in the universal currents. You will be able to decide how you can affect the operations of your life. This number carries both positive and negative attributes since no human being can carry only positive vibes.

Your life path is always permanent since it is dependent on the date of birth. Your name can always be changed but this does not change the effect of the life path number. You will need to conform to the rules set by your life path number but will always go about it in a different way.

Life path one

If your life path is the number one, you have numerous positive qualities of which leadership, self – motivation and assertiveness are a few. You are also an energetic person and always look for new projects to take on. You have a unique sense of life and are always determined to reach newer heights. You are someone who is ambitious and is always curious to learn more! While you have these many positives, there are certain negatives too! You are someone who is egocentric or passive – aggressive and may lack in self – esteem. You are arrogant and are uncooperative and can often be perceived as a bully!

Life path two

As a person with a life path number two, you will find yourself with the qualities of being sensitive, diplomatic, organized and even intuitive. You are someone who is friendly and is often at harmony that leaves you as a great mediator. You are a person who is compassionate and has the tact to deal with matters. You are someone who is loyal and intuitive. As a two, you may be shy, careless and sometimes timid. You may find yourself self – centered and will find it extremely difficult to let go of certain emotional attachments that will leave you overly sentimental. You are someone who can never work on a team and are sometimes dogmatic.

Life path three

If you are a person who has the number three, you will be charming and charismatic. When you enter a room, you will be able to create an energetic vibe that helps in drawing the crowd towards you. You are a person who is artistic, sensual, witty and intelligent. Since you have the charm, you have the confidence that helps you in communicating with the people around you. There are a few negatives to having this number as well. You are someone who is scattered and can be bored easily. You can never be trusted since your attention flits by the second who is when you leave thing s undone and expect people to clean up after you. You are someone who is insecure and is hard to understand at times.

Life path four

If you are a person with the life path four will always be reliable and is down – to – earth. You are someone who always works hard and is loyal and practical. You will be family oriented and will be systematic and methodical. You will ensure that you are a loyal person with a practical approach to life that will leave you focused. You will be someone who is arrogant and biased. Since you have a practical approach you would never choose to take another person's idea leaving you to react in ways that may sometimes be cruel and abusive. You are a person who is highly opinionated and will ensure that he has his way. You will always try your best to defend what it is that you have said or done.

Life path five

If you are someone who has the life path number five, you will be a charming person who is entertaining and is sensual. You will love freedom and are curious about understanding your thoughts. You are someone who is adventurous and is always looking at undertaking activities that are thrilling and enticing. But, there are certain negative aspects as well. You will be an irresponsible person and will find yourself over indulging in activities that will leave you unfaithful and restless. You will find yourself frustrated with life and will always be looking for something more! You may be addictive since you will tend to love activities that excite you and drive you wild!

Life Path six

If you are someone who has the life path six, you will find yourself being responsible and gentle. You will be someone who is kind, romantic and is compassionate. The best part about you is that you are someone who is very loyal and will always work towards servicing people in your community. You are someone who always works towards nurturing people and will ensure that you protect the people you love most. You are a perfectionist and a little nosy when it comes to work since you want everything to be the way you had imagined it!

You are someone who is moody and is a busybody who tries to control any given situation. You will also be someone who is somewhat smothering due to your habit to nurture and protect people.

Life path seven

As a person who has the life path seven, you will find yourself very intelligent and philosophical. You are someone who is studious and is always seeking the truth. You are a rational person and are always dignified and efficient. You are somewhat fearful and distant and try to stay aloof on most occasions and can be perceived as a snob. You are reliable but never trust another person since you do not place your faith on anybody else. You are sometimes discriminative and argumentative leaving you to close yourself off emotionally.

Life path eight

As a person with a life path number eight, you will be tenacious, focused powerful. You are someone who can always walk the talk and is a born leader. Organizing any meeting or succeeding at anything is simple for you since you are adaptable and find it easy to assume authority which will leave you in charge of the happenings in your surroundings. You are a generous person and sometimes are also a spendthrift. Since you are authoritative, you tend to become controlling and power hungry and will be easily frustrated when things do not go your way. You are stubborn and will never tolerate it when someone crosses you.

Life path nine

As a person who has the life path nine, you will find yourself to be artistic, intuitive, creative and imaginative. You will be a person who can be approached by anybody since you are easy going and exude a sense of friendliness. You are someone who is oriented towards a future and re always thorough with what you do. As a person who is caring and loving and compassionate, you find romance with ease and are quite gentle with your partner. You are someone who needs to be dependent on someone else and may sometimes lack self – confidence. You will probably begin to take on another person's problems since you are too helpful which will lead people around you to take you for a ride. You are a dreamer and may sometimes limit yourself from achieving your full potential. You sometimes procrastinate since you cannot get yourself to finish things on time.

Life path eleven

As a person with the life path eleven, you will be approachable and friendly which will leave people with a sense of calm and they will come to you like you are a plant with nectar in it and they are the bees! You are imaginative, intuitive and are hypnotic. Your charm is what brings you together with different kinds of people that feed your need for different interests. You have a superiority complex that leaves you disrespectful at times which may make you antisocial. You are someone who can be perceived to be blunt as well.

Life path twenty two

As a person with a life path numbers as twenty-two, you will find yourself charming and idealistic. You are someone who is intelligent beyond his years and will be someone who is innovative and creative. You work towards creating mass awareness and always work towards ensuring that you achieve your dream. You are tireless and will always ensure that you produce results as soon as you can. You may sometimes have the feeling of being invulnerable. You are someone who may be unfair and is selfish and could never be satiated no matter what goal you have achieved.

Life Path Cycles

Your life path is built on three cycles called the sub – cycles each of which have their very own tone of vibration. These cycles are what form the backdrop against how the vibrations in a year pan out for you. You will also be able to understand what challenges you may find yourself presented with and how you should meet and overcome those challenges. The sub paths or the life path cycles are based on the numeric values of the three components of your life path that are the birthday, month and year!

You will always have to understand how and when your life path will change. Your life path cycles all run in a sequence. They all gave a very deep connection with two cycles in astrology called the Return of the Progressed Moon and Saturn Return.

1. The formative cycle starts at the year of birth and ends at the beginning of the next cycle that is called the cycle of productivity.

2. The productive cycle begins during your first personal year and is closest to your 28th birthday. In most cases, the first personal year may fall before the 28th birthday that would imply that the beginning of the cycle is never felt until your 28th birthday. There are certain events that may correspond to the nature of the next cycle that will always be set into motion in the period of transition.

3. The harvest cycle always begins on the first personal year that is closest to your 57th birthday. In most cases, the first personal year may fall before the 57th birthday, which would imply that the beginning of the cycle is never felt until your 57th birthday. There are certain events that may correspond to the nature of the next cycle that will always be set

into motion in the period of transition. This number is called the maturity number since this is the point at which there will be changes in your life!

The sub paths are extremely important since they leave you with opportunities that help you achieve goals and also help you enjoy your personal happiness when you operate in your positive modes. When you start operating on your negative modes, you will learn some important lessons in your life, which will help you, open the positive aspects of your life. When these cycles change, people tend to mysteriously switch from one career path to the next since they have a different way of living life at the moment. They have certain expectations and find it difficult to live the way they used to. They also change the way they live.

Kundalini

Kundalini Rising – What Is It?

Kundalini Rising (a.k.a. Kundalini Awakening) is based on the idea that all humans contain some sort of energy within the base of their spine called "Kundalini". The idea is that through vigorous meditation and yoga, this energy can be "Awakened" and thus travel up and down the spine through the body. This energy is often represented as a coiled snake at the base of the spine, which matches with its name which roughly translates into "coiled". The results of this awakening are said to cause states of extreme bliss and enlightenment. To reach this period, it is said that the Kundalini needs to pass through several chakra points inside the human body and along the spine. It is believed that once this energy is awakened, it does not ever return to its coiled state but will ebb and flow throughout the lifetime of that individual.

Kundalini in History

The roots of the Kundalini idea trace their way back to Ancient India, in the Indus Valley, Ancient Egypt, and Sumerian civilizations. Most notably we can see this in the Ancient Vedic texts in which numerous Rig-Veda hymns praise a liquid known as "Soma" that many believe to be a metaphor for this energy within us all. Kundalini has strong ties with the ancient god known as Lord Shiva, for Lord Shiva is always seen with a serpent wrapped around his neck which some argue represents Kundalini. Possibly the most notable allegorical record of Kundalini is an ancient Ramayana tale which tells the tale of a noble and his beautiful wife. In this tale, the noble, who goes by the name Rama, and his wife, who goes by the name Sita, are caught in escort with an evil demon called Ravana. Ravana kidnaps Sita, who is meant to encapsulate the ideal woman and perfect femininity, and imprisons her in an island fortress called "Lanka". It is well known within this tale that Lanka is meant to represent a physical human body and Sita is meant to represent the Kundalini energy. Ravana, on the other hand, is meant to represent the five senses and the five organs of action which are believed to lead man towards desire and away from their spirituality. He represents this symbolically with his ten heads. Rama is meant to represent the consciousness, and through powerful expertise, "releases" Sita, a very clear metaphor for the releasing of Kundalini within a human.

Kundalini Yoga

Yoga, in recent years, has come to the forefront of modern physical fitness. With its image as the skinny girl who can do the splits and balance perfectly with her leg over her head, it has become a very popular form of physical workout. While Kundalini Yoga does offer some form of physical exertion, it has a taste of spirituality to go along with it. Kundalini Yoga is often performed with a more worship-like air about it. Often taking place in almost complete silence and rarely in a gym, this workout is definitely different from many others. One of these differences is its vast spiritual history. This yoga is old and has managed to stay with almost the same principles for centuries. This is partially due to the fact that Kundalini does not have any overwhelming strict or suffocating dogmas to steer away practitioners. Kundalini allows itself not to be a strict religion but simply to be a tool one can use to find their inner spirituality. In ancient times, yoga was not confined by the definition of physical activity but, in fact, was considered simply a connection to one's spiritual self through their bodies. They had no goals of physical fitness but rather a connection to the energy they believe lives within us all – and for this connection, they stressed the fact that no buffer was necessary. No prayer or food or special dance – simply to practice and focus. In fact, it is recorded that the first Kundalini sessions consisted of almost entirely no physical activity whatsoever. Disciples simply sat in front of their master and listened to their revelations about spirit. This practice was very common in Ancient Vedic times and was later replicated in religious figures known as Buddha and Jesus. Throughout the years, this method of spirituality evolved until it began to include the physical acting out of the spiritual visions. This then evolved into what we know as yoga today. One of the reasons that this form of spiritual expression is not commonly known or spoken of today is due to its secretiveness throughout history. For thousands of years, the study of Kundalini was kept secret and sacred, known only by an inner group of spiritualists and their students. This was often explained through the idea that the public was not ready or prepared for such incredible knowledge and that the awakening of Kundalini amongst the average folk would cause chaos and destruction. Kundalini would still be mostly lost to western society if not for the teachings of a man known as "Yogi Bahjan". Yogi chose to impart his wisdom upon the youth of the United States due to the uprising of the hippie movement in the late 1960s. He came to America and found hundreds of youth desperately wanting to be closer to their spiritual side and going about it in all the wrong ways through drugs and mysticism. He taught over 8,000 yoga classes. At the beginning of his career, he is also credited with establishing the Healthy, Happy, Holy Organization. Without this man, Kundalini Yoga and subsequent Awakening would never have reached the States.

Kundalini Rising and You

Now that you fully understand the origins of Kundalini and how it has reached us, it is time to learn how you too can awaken the energy within. With the internet today, anyone can find hundreds and hundreds of ways to awaken the energy within them. However, the average person must approach these with caution, as this energy is extremely powerful, and without the learned expertise, over time they may harm themselves or their chakra balances.

Warning: we highly recommend that the reader consults with an expert regarding the awakening of their energy for their life before attempting to do so.

1) The first step to awakening your chakra energy is to practice mindful breathing exercises. To begin, you will want to relax and take several cleansing breaths in and out. You will want to begin to practice a sort of soft abdominal breathing – these are soft, calm breaths within you that eventually bring your abdomen and lungs to an equilibrium of gases.

2) Now, you will want to find with your mind's eye (this is easiest done with your eyes closed) the location of your kidneys. This may sound strange, but you simply have to visualize it in the lower back of your body are your two kidneys. Visualize them and imagine their location.

3) You will want to "massage" the kidneys by releasing several breaths of air that expel all the air from your lungs and the bag within your abdomen.

4) At this point, to help with your breathing, you will want to begin chanting the phrase "Num Mum Yum Pa 'Hum." As you exhale, you will want to focus and try to feel for the vibration of the right Adrenal, the Right Kidney and then the subsequent left Adrenal or Left Kidney.

5) If you are having difficulty feeling the vibration in your kidneys, you can rub your lower back to promote the activity.

6) You will now want to make sure that you are in a comfortable position.

7) You will physically want to lift your arms above your head with your thumbs out. You will want to make sure your shoulders are rotated down and back. Rotating your thumbs back and forth, you should be able to feel the connection of your thumbs to your lungs.

8) You will now want to reach your index finger towards the sky and feel the large intestine connect to the ribcage.

9) You will want to lift your collarbones and feel a responding suspension of the kidneys.

10) Think back with your mind's eye to the airbags and their connection to the kidneys.

11) You will now want to tuck the chin and release a small bit of air from the diaphragm.

12) Inhale deeply, feel the air bags, and make sure that the chin, tongue, palate, and sinuses are stacked neatly with a connection to the spinal cord.

13) Exhale slowly. You should feel the top of your lungs buoy upwards.

14) Inhale again touching the top of the chest and bottom of the abdomen.

15) Exhale and feel the chakra point at the top of the nose.

16) Breathe again, letting the chakra point expand.

17) Feel the vertebrae of your spinal cord lift and extend upwards slightly.

Practicing this meditation system on a regular basis can help guide you to your own Kundalini Awakening.

Now we will describe some of the common side effects and positive as well as negative experiences of those who have awakened their own energy within themselves. Kundalini energy is often described as a sensation of electricity or internal lightning bolts within the person at the sight of the awakening. People are often described to shake or jerk their body parts or limbs. This is usually completely out of the control of the individual who is awakening their energy. You may also feel upon the awakening of this energy a sensation of insects crawling along your spinal cord, along with feelings of either intense heat or intense cold. The individual in question may also feel an intense moment of pleasure that sometimes leads to an orgasmic state. They also may experience sudden and unexplainable mood swings, far beyond normal highs and lows. As a result of this awakening, people often report having much more empathetic bonds with those around them. They have also said that this increased level of empathy results in telepathic or psychic abilities. Aging has been said to slow as a result of the rising of Kundalini as well as the increase in creative ability and charismatic personality traits. These individuals often say that the great mysteries of life are no longer mysteries; they are connected more deeply to all that is and ever was.

An individual in search of the enlightenment that comes with the awakening of Kundalini is strongly urged to consult with professionals and support groups on the matter. Trying to find an experienced Kundalini yoga instructor who has experienced an awakening themselves will greatly help someone who's desire it is to awaken this incredible power. Attempting to awaken this power on your own can result in terrible consequences as well as simply not working at all. Many support groups can be found online, and Kundalini Yoga instructors are common in larger cities. If you have trouble finding one in your local area, many online instructors openly give their knowledge to the public. They can be found on YouTube, Pinterest, and blog sites. Many YouTube videos have been made on the process of awakening the Kundalini as well as how to cope with the aftermath. If you have experienced an awakening or would like to, we would highly recommend searching through these.

Kundalini Yoga Poses

Kundalini yoga poses are also called asanas. Asanas generally apply pressure on your nerves and acupressure points in your body, which reflexes to the brain and body to allow for certain effects. These poses are generally to help with stimulating the organs and glands for better body awareness.

(Sukhasana) Easy Pose

To perform the easy pose, cross feet allowing your ankles to touch, or place both feet flat on the floor. Press your bottom most point of your spine up and keep your back straight.

(Siddhasana) Perfect Pose

Start with sukasana and at the perineum, press into it with the heel on your right foot, the sole of your foot should be resting on the left upper thigh. Place the heel of your left foot over the top of the right foot so that you are pressing upward with your toes tucked between the thigh and calf muscle. Your knees should be resting on the ground with your heels directly above one another. This is the most comfortable asana position and is considered to be the one to promote the most psychic power.

(Padmasana) Lotus Pose

Starting with the easy pose, lift your left foot up and onto the upper part of the thigh on your right leg. Then your left foot should be resting on the upper part of your left thigh. Make sure to keep them near your body as possible. This is a safe posture that is simpler than it sounds, and it is a good way to enhance deep meditative states. Make sure that you always have your right leg on top.

(Vajrasana) Rock Pose

Kneel, sitting on the back of your heels. The top of your feet should be flat on the floor. Make sure that the heels are pressing into the nerves that are positioned in the middle of your rear end. They called this the rock pose because of its help in the digestive process.

Hero (Celibate) Pose

Along with your feet positioned equidistant to your hips, go down on your knees and sit in sandwiched between your feet. Hero (celibate) pose helps channel sensual power up the spinal column.

Deep Breathing Techniques (Pranayama)

For practitioners of Kundalini that have been doing the deep breathing techniques for many years, it is a natural thing that occurs for them. A lot of the time, a newer student will fill the lower abdomen area of the lungs and then try to fill the chest area but do not keep the right pressure, and the complete breath is only obtained in the chest cavity. This is not the diaphragm breathing that is needed.

Long Deep Breathing

Long deep breathing is a good way to relax and is often the first breathing technique that is taught when starting Kundalini. This also helps those who have lung-related issues with building up their lung capacity.

You begin by sitting with your legs crossed. You then take in a deep breath filling the abdominal area by pushing the air downward, then pressing the air into the lower areas. By arching your body somewhat forward and resting your palms on your knees, your chest cavity can begin to open forward. This allows you to keep pressure on the lungs and the abdominal area.

Once your lungs have been completely filled, hold the breath for a moment while pushing your shoulders back to expand the chest outward. You should feel the full pressure of the diaphragm at this point. Once you feel this, contract your diaphragm and push out the air.

The purpose of breathing this way through the nose for several of these breaths is to help the flow of energy and consciousness. This also helps with the blood circulation because of the involvement of the lungs and the deep breaths that circulate through them.

Once this type of deep breathing has been accomplished several times, you will find that it becomes a lot more natural. You will also begin to feel the motion that the entire diaphragm is involved during the whole breathing cycle.

Breath of Fire (Agni-Prasanna)

The breath of fire is an energizing breath that is cleansing to the body, and that is powered through spasms of the abdomen.

Once the long deep breathing technique has been mastered and you can feel the diaphragm, then you can begin the breath of fire technique. This begins with the long deep breathing technique. Once you take the air in, you do not hold; you immediately let it out. Once it has been let out, you immediately bring in another breath. You keep doing this process. It is reminiscent of a locomotive engine lurching on the tracks.

With each breath, you replace it with another until a nice rhythm begins to form out of the breathing. The breath of fire is meant to help charge the nervous system. It allows your glands to secrete the hormones you need and the blood to purify. Using this breathing technique for periods of time can help strengthen the mind and allows the body to become more connected to the mind.

The Language of Energy

Astrology is self-considered to be the language of energy that is exerted by the Planets, Elements, Signs, houses, and aspects. The astrological birth chart of an individual shows the pattern of energy which influences them in doing work and progress. Often the exaltation of energy may have a negative impact on the personality of an individual. Each element, sign, Planet, houses exert vibrant energy which is experienced by an individual such:

The Planets regulate the flow of energy and their dimensions in which this energy is experienced.

The Signs in the zodiac wheel show the pattern of energy and the quality of energy experienced by an individual

The Elements like Air, Fire, Earth, and Water considered as the substance of energy.

The houses in the zodiac wheel represent the field in which these energies were experienced.

The energy that we experience is directly reflected in the personality of an individual's life. The energy can be malefic or beneficial means it can be constructive or destructive. In astrology, we deal with different energies and their interaction and mutual relation with the other pattern of energy. The birth chart or an astrological chart shows the precise form of energy and its nature for us. Astrology is concerned with the three basic forms of energy which are as follows;

- The Constellation's energy by which the Sun is posited during the time of birth.
- The ascendant energy or the rising sign energy is where a man responses.
- The physical form of energy is the one governed by the Moon.
- The energy of a particular sign with which a person is born has a great significance on its own.

- The energy act as an indicator of present problems that are related to the quality of the individual. It expresses the activity during the incarnation and governs the fact (if I could express it), whereas, the ascendant/rising sign shows the flow of energy in the line used to fulfill the desires and governs the fact that (of course I can do it if handled rightly).

- The power also holds future secrets and symbolizes the understanding which can be utilized to solve the problems and achieve success. It shows positive, vibrant energy.

The Moon exerts a steady-state form of energy which uses inertia. It indicates the body type and quality of energy, which pushes the person towards goals. The energy comes from the experience which is expressed physically.

The month of birth is indicative of the opportunity in which the soul comes into existence with the quality of energy and nature of the force to be experienced from that. Though the energy is neither destructive, it will start from the same end where you have left.

The energy of the Sun in the solar system has vital importance. It exerts a type of force which pushes you to the extent of origin and beginning just like a flower comes out the bud. Thus, considering the birth chart of an individual location of Planets, Signs, the ascendants, and house. These all speak in the form of energy which exerts its influence in the person's life. Considering the circle of the solar system on which our horoscope is based affects the soul, which is considered as the point of spiritual energy also. The sign falls in particular Elements like Earth, Fire, Air, and Water. These are the thoughts to be the person living below the diaphragm that use the energy of the lower body parts to perceive life.

The meditation also developed the energy from the inner soul which can be used for spiritual connection and turns into the positive vibes and by mantric words that can be used by the person in governing the power of their soul in a positive way.

To an extent when the energy of two different constellations collides in the same sign or house, then the person has two different forms of energies which sometimes creates complications and also makes a smoother life. In the modern astrological concept, physical and spiritual energy is the keywords of the astrological chart.

Thus, the point to be noticed is that astrology is self-concerned about the language of energy. The energy is directly concerned with the work form, which has to be done to fulfill the desires and our role in the physical as well as spiritual life.

The Test Enneagram Instructions

There are many Enneagram tests available online. Whatever Enneagram test you decide to take, the most important thing that you must do is to read the instructions carefully before you complete the test. Just like any other exam, an Enneagram test is very important, but it is also fun and stimulating.

The following nine paragraphs give a full description of each of the different personality types. No personality type is considered to be superior to the others, and each description represents a simple snapshot of each personality type on the Enneagram. Note that no paragraph is intended to give a deeper description of an individual type than the others.

Carefully read through each description and select three paragraphs that you agree fit your individual personality best. Once you have identified these three paragraphs, number them in order of the most fitting to the least fitting description of you. That is, the one the describes you best ranks 1 and the least ranks 3. These are the three that are highly likely to contribute to your personality.

Note that each one of the nine descriptions may be like you to a certain extent but select only the three that are most like you. It is important that you consider each paragraph as a whole rather than dismissing it all together by just reading a single sentence.

Before selecting a paragraph, ask yourself, "Is this paragraph a better description of me than the others?"

You may find it difficult to select three paragraphs. In this case, think about what a close friend would say when describing you. Remember that personality patterns are often quite evident in adult life.

How to record your selection: Once you have read, understood, and selected the three paragraphs that best describe you, record them as first choice, second choice, and third choice. Then refer to the answers below to determine what personality type is represented in each paragraph.

Enneagram Test

These are the nine Enneagram descriptions for the nine essential personality types.

A. I approach things that really matter to me with an all-or-nothing method. I place emphasis mainly on strength, honesty, and reliability. In other words, what you see is what you get in return. I find it hard to trust people easily until they have proven themselves to be dependable. I prefer when people are straight up with me. I can tell when someone is being cunning, exploitative, or lying. I struggle with weaknesses in people unless I completely understand the reason underlying their weaknesses, or when they are striving to overcome them.

I find it hard to follow people's directives, especially when I have no respect for their authority. I prefer taking charge myself. When I am angry, I display my feelings and am always ready to stand up for my friends and family in unjust conditions. I may not win every fight, but people know that I have been there, done that!

B. I have high standards of correctness and I expect people to abide by those standards. It is quite easy for me to see when things are going wrong and find ways to improve the situation. People often perceive me as being overly critical and a perfectionist. However, I find it hard to overlook things when they are not being handled in the right way. I take responsibility for all things assigned to me and am sure to do them right.

Often, I resent people when they fail to do things the right way or act irresponsibly/unfairly. In such a case, I do not show them my opinions openly. I prioritize work over pleasure; I often suppress my selfish interests to ensure that work gets done.

C. I see people's points of view with ease. Because of my ability to perceive both pros and cons of something, sometimes I may come across as indecisive. Being able to appreciate both sides of a situation lets me help people resolve conflicts. However, this same ability makes me aware of how people's personal priorities, agendas, and positions differ from mine.

I become easily distracted and I get off course from the things am trying to achieve. When this happens, I concern myself with things that are trivial. I find it difficult to determine what is important. To avoid conflicts, I choose to agree with the majority; because of this people consider me to be easy-going, agreeable, and people-pleasing. It takes a lot of effort to get me to show my anger at someone in a direct way.

D. I am sensitive about people's feelings, and I can perceive their needs even if they don't open up to me. It can be frustrating to know what people need because I am not able to do as much for them as I want. I easily say yes to people and wish that sometimes I would say no; I often end up using so much effort and energy taking care of others that I forget to take care of myself.

It hurts me when people think that my actions mean that I am manipulative or controlling, I am just trying to understand them so that I can better help. I like it when people consider me to be warmhearted and kind. If not, I become demanding and emotional. Good relationships are very important to me, and I strive to make them happen.

E. I am strongly motivated to be the best at what I do. Because of this, I have received lots of recognition for my accomplishments over the years. I ensure that I do a lot and I am always successful at everything I do. I strongly identify with what I do, mainly because I consider success and recognition as measures of self-worth. I take on more tasks than will fit in the time available. When that happens, I push aside my feelings so that I can concentrate on getting things done.

Because I always have something to do, I do not have time to sit around or be idle. I grow impatient when people waste my time. In some cases, I prefer taking over a task that someone else is doing because they are going too slow for my liking. I feel good when I stay "on top of things." While I like working independently to complete tasks, I am also a great team player.

F. I consider myself quiet and analytical. I prefer spending more time alone than most people. When people are engaging in conversations or discussions, I prefer being an observer rather than taking part. I don't like it when people place too many expectations on me. I get in touch with my inner person and feelings alone better than when I am in a crowd or with people.

I don't get bored when I am alone because I possess a strong mental life. I protect my time and energy, which allows me to live a simple life without complications, thus feeling self-sufficient.

G. I possess a vivid imagination, especially concerning matters to do with safety and security. I can spot danger and harm from afar and this triggers extreme fear, as though it were happening in real time. I either face danger or try to avoid it. Because of my imagination, I have a good sense of humor.

I would prefer if life were full of certainty, but this makes me doubt the people around me. When someone is sharing their views, I can see disadvantages and pitfalls and this makes people consider me to be someone who are very astute.

I'm always suspicious of authority and am uncomfortable when people see me as an authority. When I commit myself to something or someone, I am very loyal.

H. People consider me a very optimistic person. I enjoy creating new interests and ideas of things to do. My mind is very active and I am constantly analyzing different ideas. I like to have a big picture of how the ideas I come up with fit together. I get excited when concepts connect eventually, even when they seemed not to at first. I devote a lot of effort and energy into the things that interest me and find it very hard to stick to things that are unrewarding, including routine tasks.

I prefer being part of a project at the very inception, during planning and implementation because these things are interesting. However, once my interest is exhausted, I find it difficult to stay focused, and I move on to the next thing that captivates me. If something lowers my mood, I prefer focusing on things that bring me pleasure because I believe everyone deserves an enjoyable life.

I. I am a very sensitive person and possess some intense feelings. I feel different from other people, and most of them misunderstand me or alienate me as a loner. Others consider my behavior to be dramatic. People criticize me as being overly sensitive. Inside, I have a nostalgia to connect with people emotionally and establish a sense of belonging and relationship. I often want what I cannot have, and this makes it hard for me to appreciate the uniqueness of each relationship.

My quest for emotional connection has been my desire my whole life. The absence of this is the reason I get melancholic and depressed. I often wonder why people have much better, healthier, and happier relationships than I do.

Enneagram Test Outcome

Which three of the above paragraphs best describe your personality?

These are the outcomes of each of the paragraph descriptions above. Use this table to identify what personality type you are.

- A-Type 8
- B-Type 1
- C-Type 9
- D-Type 2
- E-Type 3
- F-Type 5
- G-Type 6
- H-Type 7
- I-Type 4

Decoding the Nine-Value Code

LIFE TABLES

Own energy

1. Energy draws from other sources, often beyond measure. A refined egoist. Physically weak, quickly tired.

2. Close to the egoist (all the time he praises himself as if for sale).

3. Good, compliant character.

4. Sometimes compliant, but more often achieves the goal.

5. Strong-willed, strong character.

6. It seems that you are a dictator, a very strong-willed character.

7. A person is cruel, but at the same time for the loved one can do the impossible. It's very difficult with him.

Energy from nature, bioenergy.

0. This person has a good attitude towards others, is very responsive to changes in atmospheric pressure, often prone to colds.

1. Hypersensitivity to atmospheric phenomena, it is advisable to go in for sports, a contrast shower is useful.

2. Bioenergy is enough. It rarely happens without mood.

3. The tendency to extrasensory perception.

4. People around them are drawn. Their presence softens the atmosphere. They react to changes in atmospheric phenomena. They can be good doctors, masseurs. If you don't give this energy away, frequent headaches can bother you.--

5. A person can develop remarkable strength, but if you do not physically engage, energy can move into another sphere.-

6. A person can develop remarkable strength, but if you do not engage physically, energy can move into another sphere. It has a great energy effect on others, subordinating them to their will.-

The energy of space

0. A man likes to talk, moderately accurate. It is difficult for him to give exact sciences.

1. Man of mood (I want to do, I want not).

2. Propensity for exact sciences.

3. Remarkable physicists, mathematicians, chemists, a humanitarian bias is possible.-

4. Intuition can be the meaning of life. These people often anticipate events, a good analytical mind.

Health energy

There is no health energy. A painful condition, especially with a small amount of bioenergy.

1. The tendency to disease in old age.

2. Health is normal and even elevated temperament.

3. The body will be resistant to physical illnesses, but the psyche may be weak.

4. Excellent health.

Energy of intuition:

A person is always trying to do something, to prove something, always a head in thought, himself in an experiment. Life experience shows that many mistakes will be made by this person. All that is given to him - he "punches his head."--

1. The channel of intuition is open; these people make fewer mistakes in decision making.

2. Good intuition. You can be an investigator, a lawyer. Rarely mistaken.

3. Almost clairvoyant, these people know what they are doing.

4. Clairvoyants, everything that is happening around them is clear to them and do not try to convince them. There are times when they are outside of space and spatial time.--

Energy performance, grounding.

There is no tendency to physical labor. Physical work is performed as necessary, and not as desired.

1. A man loves physical labor, he needs it, but you can think about learning.

2. Love of physical labor.

3. Very charming, elevated temperament, a person cannot live without physical labor. Your partner should be with lots of bioenergy.-

4. A man works a lot. For him there is no severity of labor (physical), he always works.

The energy of talent.

It's hard for a person to live and earn money, talent will come in subsequent transformations.

1. A capable, inventive person. There is talent, but dimly expressed. Endowed with artistic and musical taste.-

2. If you develop abilities, then a person is musical, has a good artistic taste, draws well, and is endowed with everything: bad and good. There will be no closed doors for him. From childhood, you need to prepare yourself to disinterestedly act in favor of others, regardless of your personal interests.

3. You have to face serious difficulties.

4. You should remember caution.

Energy binding.

A person is not always punctual and obligatory.

1. A person with a developed sense of duty. Mandatory, punctual.-

2. A sense of duty is very developed, there is always a desire to help.

3. A very big responsibility, service to the people.

4. A person with parapsychological abilities, with knowledge of the exact sciences.-

The energy of the mind.

1. Mental abilities can make themselves felt in the second half of life, after accumulating experience.

2. As a rule, these people can easily study and there is no need to "cram" the material.-

3. From birth, a smart head, but reluctantly learns.

4. Smart by nature, everything is given to him.

5. A rare mind, but rudeness and mercy interfere.

Conclusion

Now, as you have to go through, now you will come to know how you can read and construct your natal charts and their deeper meanings. This must have explained all the basics of astrology; the history and origin of the astrology make you familiar with the concept of astrological predictions. It has explained all the related tools of astrology that is used by the astrologer for making a prediction. If you are a beginner, you will be able to deal with the astrological aspect.

The main aim of this was to make you aware of the basic concept of astrology and how to use them in the prediction of an individual's birth chart and their personality. It has explained all the possible facts of astrology that you people like the most. I am sure this will definitely help you in learning astrology in a better and easy way.

As you all that the celestial objects present in the universe emit different kind of energy which is directly or indirectly concerned with our daily life activity but mostly, we are not aware of these and neglected by us most of the time. The purpose of this is to tell you about the techniques and tools that are used in astrology to predict the circumstances in your life. The content of this opens your eyes towards the astrological aspects and meaning of each and every celestial object in your life.

The Enneagram sheds light on self-awareness and personal growth. Considering this is a new year, make the decision to look deep inside yourself for the things you like most and the things you would like to change to be a better version of yourself. Learning about your Enneagram personality type is an excellent catalyst to making a positive change in your life. So, what is it going to be for you in 2020? Take a bold step and make a difference in your life. You will thank the Enneagram for aiding in successful personal growth later.

The more that you invest in understanding yourself through crafts like numerology, the easier it is for you to develop yourself along this journey. It is important to understand that tools like numerology are only meant to be used as a guide and not as a strict rule in your life. As you read through your chart and reflect on it, remember that you may find areas where you do not resonate with your chart simply because you are a unique individual. You may find that you can find an even deeper resonance by going back to the double-digit number before the single digit number to help you resonate even deeper. In other numbers, you may completely identify with the primary number and find that it tells you plenty. To summarize, there is so much to be learned about yourself through numerology, but the ultimate learning comes from reflecting on it and seeing how it actually relates to you in your lifetime. This way, you can learn not only about numerology, but about yourself, too.

It is a good idea to write your chart down on paper or in a document so that you can reflect back on it whenever you need to. Many people find that their charts become valuable to them at many points in life, and they reference back to it frequently. As a result, they are able to get great information about how they can move through different phases of their life, what they can expect from the people around them, and how they make better decisions. Regularly reflecting back on your chart can be a valuable opportunity for you to move in alignment with your true soul, which is the biggest benefit of numerology.

Printed in Great Britain
by Amazon